P9-BAW-353

SUCCEEDING WITH
STANDARDS

Linking Curriculum, Assessment, and Action Planning

Judy F. Carr and
Douglas E. Harris

Association for Supervision and Curriculum Development
Alexandria, Virginia USA

OUACHITA TECHNICAL COLLEGE

Association for Supervision and Curriculum Development
1703 N. Beauregard St. • Alexandria, VA 22311-1714 USA
Telephone: 1-800-933-2723 or 703-578-9600 • Fax: 703-575-5400
Web site: http://www.ascd.org • E-mail: member@ascd.org

Copyright © 2001 by Judy F. Carr and Douglas E. Harris. All rights reserved. No part of this publication may be reproduced or transmitted in any form or by any means, electronic or mechanical, including photocopy, recording, or any information storage and retrieval system, without permission from the authors.

ASCD publications present a variety of viewpoints. The views expressed or implied in this book should not be interpreted as official positions of the Association.

Printed in the United States of America.

April 2001 member book (pcr). ASCD Premium, Comprehensive, and Regular members periodically receive ASCD books as part of their membership benefits. No. FY01-06.

ASCD Product No. 101005
ASCD member price: $20.95   nonmember price: $24.95

Library of Congress Cataloging-in-Publication Data
Carr, Judy F.
  Succeeding with standards : linking curriculum, assessment, and action
planning / Judy F. Carr and Douglas E. Harris.
      p. cm.
Includes bibliographical references (p.   ) and index.
  ISBN 0-87120-509-2 (alk. paper)
  1. Education—Standards—United States. 2. Curriculum
planning—United States. 3. Educational tests and measurements—United
States. I. Harris, Douglas E. II. Title.
  LB3060.83 .C37 2001
  379.1'58'0973—dc21
                                                                2001000694

07 06 05 04 03 02 01   10 9 8 7 6 5 4 3 2 1

LB
5060.83
.C37
2001

Succeeding with Standards: Linking Curriculum, Assessment, and Action Planning

1

Overview of Standards Linking

In many schools and districts, the local curriculum is a hodge-podge of individual initiatives knit together by collective good intentions. Administrators and teachers often purchase materials, convene committees, and create curriculum guides with little attention to the relationship of each piece to the whole. Educators act without proper data to guide their decisions, without grounding in research and best practice, and without a plan for turning their vision into reality.

We all know this kind of approach does not work. Overall student performance is inconsistent. Students don't learn as well as they might, and we have little assurance that all children are getting their rightful opportunities to learn. Standards alone cannot change these realities. Instead, successful change occurs when all aspects of the local curriculum are linked to standards through a purposeful, coherent system of processes and products.

The Vision

Standards must be put into practice at all levels of the system before they can make a significant difference for students. Standards are especially important in the classroom, which is where

1

they ultimately effect the most change. National, state, and local standards are important resources for teachers, but these standards have little meaning until teachers and administrators take true ownership of them. For example, will the local district adopt state standards, adapt standards from national professional organizations (such as the National Council of Teachers of Mathematics), or create new, locally specific standards using other documents as resources? Other important questions include

- Which standards are the focus for student learning?
- Can any one student achieve the complete set of standards?
- Are the standards presented in a form that is useful to and usable by teachers?
- How should the standards to be used in classrooms and schools throughout the school district?

Without decisions on questions like these, the local curriculum vision will be distorted, with teachers referring to different resources. Administrators, teachers, students, parents, and the community need a clear vision of what is expected in terms of student learning. Clarity is achieved when districts and schools formally identify their standards and then use them consistently throughout the curriculum process.

We have created a standards linking system for use with local curriculums. Figure 1.1 shows the components of this system, which encompasses 11 important areas, including a vision and an action plan.

In most states and local districts, standards are written for each subject area by committees of experts who focus on one area of the curriculum. Using committees of experts certainly assures content accuracy and breadth, but it leads to a fragmented curriculum vision if no one evaluates the cumulative effect of the standards.

FIGURE 1.1

The Process of Standards Linking

The 11 components of standards linking are listed below. The process of standards linking is recursive and the list indicates logic, not the order, of the components.

Vision
What are the standards, evidence, and learning opportunities
to which the school or district is committed?

Current State
Who is currently teaching what standards and evidence?
What is the nature of the instruction?
Who is currently assessing what standards and evidence? By what means?

Curriculum and Assessment Plan
Who is responsible for teaching what standards and evidence?
What should instruction look like?
What is to be assessed? By whom? By what means?

School Decisions
Through what courses, topics, and themes will the standards and evidence plan be taught and assessed?
Do all students have opportunities to be instructed and assessed in relation to the standards?

Resources
What is needed in the way of funding, expertise, and materials?

Professional Development Plan
What do teachers need to know and be able to do in order to teach and assess?
How will opportunities to address these needs be provided over time?

Supervision and Evaluation
What supports and feedback will teachers receive as they work to implement the curriculum?
Who is responsible for providing what?
What documentation is needed?

Student Profile
What assessment information will be kept on each student, K–12?

Comprehensive Assessment System
How will the local curriculum be assessed?
What sources of data will be included?

Reporting
What information is needed by what audiences?
How will it be provided?

Action Plan
What do we need to do to improve student learning?

Source: The Center for Curriculum Renewal, 1999

When all the history a child ought to know is added to all the science that is important—and then both of those subject areas are added to all the English, mathematics, social studies, physical education, and arts he ought to know—the result is an overwhelming mass of knowledge. One student cannot realistically attain all of this knowledge in the course of a K–12 education. Educators don't take these conglomerations of standards seriously. Even worse, individual teachers start to make different decisions about which standards to teach and which to ignore. Such idiosyncratic decisions erode the standards and lead to inconsistent programs with no basis in standards at all.

Even when various sets of standards encompass a realistic scope, having to refer to separate documents can lead to logistical difficulties for teachers who must implement multiple sets of standards. A way to alleviate this problem is to abstract standards and republish them by grade levels or grade-level clusters. For example, South Carolina wanted middle school teachers to use the state's standards to design interdisciplinary units. To achieve this goal, the state created an edited version of several sets of standards. As a result, teachers use only one document in their work, not seven separate documents. Local districts can create similar resources that make the standards clear and accessible for every teacher. (The process of developing the local curriculum is further described in the next chapter.)

Once a school or district commits to a set of standards—and everyone understands what "our" standards are—it must specify how the standards will be used. This step requires intentional planning for teaching, learning, assessment, resources, professional development, supervision and evaluation of the instructional process, and program evaluation in the form of a comprehensive, standards-based assessment system.

The school board should formally adopt a plan that puts this standards-based assessment system into policy. Then this plan should be used as the basis for decisions in the many areas described throughout this book. A critical first step is to evaluate the current status of curriculum, instruction, and assessment in relation to the standards.

Current State

Typically, standards reinforce the best practice of the best teachers. As you begin to look at current work with standards, you will likely find that you can retain much of teachers' current practice along with curriculum documents that have already been revised in response to standards. You will find that some standards are being taught but not assessed, assessed but not taught, or inconsistently taught and assessed within or across grade levels.

Before making specific plans for local curriculum, instruction, and assessment, you must answer these critical questions about your current work with standards:

- Who is currently teaching what standards?
- What is the nature of the instruction?
- Who is currently assessing what standards? By what means?

This process is different from the conventional "curriculum mapping" designed by Fenwick English (English, 1992) because the focus here is on linkage with identified standards. The questions are no longer "Who is teaching what topics?" or "What materials are being used?" Instead, the questions are "Who is teaching to what standards?" "What form does the instruction take?" and "Who is assessing what standards and by what means?" Teachers sometimes must go through a toilsome process to provide this information, but the power of accessing and revising such a database far outweighs the initial drudgery of putting the information together.

The Essex Town Supervisory Union in Essex, Vermont, was one of the first districts to use technology as a tool in this process. After adapting the state's standards, they published *Essex Town Supervisory Union Standards*. Then the administrative team, teacher leaders, and school board wanted to know where the district stood with regard to implementation of standards. What was happening that could be acknowledged and celebrated? What was not happening that indicated a need for change?

The district was large enough that they could use a sampling system to collect data from teachers. Then all teachers checked a draft report for errors and oversights. For each standard and related evidence (local language for the equivalent of content standards and performance standards), teachers entered what they taught, what they assessed, and how they taught and assessed into a computer database. An analysis of the database showed that some items were taught and assessed by all teachers at a grade level. Some items were taught by some teachers at the grade level but not others. Some items were not taught or assessed by anyone; some standards were taught but not assessed, and, interestingly, some were assessed but not taught. The database enabled teachers and administrators to look from one grade level to another to track continuity of instruction and assessment (or lack thereof) across grade levels.

For each subject area, a committee drafted observations and recommendations related to the findings of this standards-linking study. Then the teachers reviewed the findings, observations, and recommendations before they began making decisions about change. This focus shifted their conversations from "what I do versus what you do" to a shared problem-solving context that considered questions such as, "Does it matter that 'X' is taught in 2nd grade but not assessed until 4th? Should all teachers teach 'Y'? How do you assess 'Z' in your classroom?" Ultimately, these conversations lead to meaningful and sustained reform in curriculum, instruction, and assessment. A database process of deciding who is responsible for teaching and assessing what standards retains the best of the current system and clarifies what needs to change to improve students' learning in relation to standards.

The Curriculum and Assessment Plan

Unlike separate curriculum guides, a curriculum and assessment plan clearly articulates responsibility for teaching and assessing standards for student learning. Figure 1.2 describes seven characteristics of a curriculum and assessment plan.

Once you have accurate information about what standards are being taught and assessed throughout the district, you can decide what *should* be taught and assessed in which grade levels, through what courses, and by what means. Clearly designate where all standards and evidence of performance will be taught and assessed. Most schools find it is easiest to start with standards that are already consistently taught and assessed at particular grade levels or in particular courses. Then they move to the standards that are taught by the majority of teachers and then work on standards that are not taught or assessed at all. As a final step, review all decisions to determine:

- Is this the best plan?
- Do students have adequate opportunity to learn and perform in relation to the standards?
- Are multiple measures used to assess student learning?
- Are the standards revisited frequently enough to lead to solid learning?

- Is the plan efficient? Is anything ignored or overemphasized?

Once these decisions are made, you can become more explicit about the types of assessments that will be used. Eventually you can link selection of resources to standards-based learning and assessment. Begin collecting examples of staff and student work for a process of benchmarking that shows everyone in the school community what good teaching and learning truly looks like.

Instructional Guidelines

If all students are to attain the standards identified in the district's vision, then certain practices, procedures, and programs must be in place. Instructional guidelines describe good practice,

---

FIGURE 1.2

Characteristics of a Curriculum and Assessment Plan

The following seven characteristics of a curriculum and assessment plan were developed using standards linking.

Characteristic	Description
Explicit	Expresses clear targets for learning drawn from the identified standards.
Coherent	Organizes content (concepts, skills, and processes) to show increasingly rigorous expectations as students move to higher grades.
Dynamic	Supports rich interactions among the standards, learner strengths and needs, effective instruction, and multidimensional assessment.
Practical	Provides a clear, well-organized, user-friendly format.
Comprehensive	Incorporates all subject areas that are part of the curriculum.
Coherent	Uses consistent organizational approaches and language across subject areas throughout the document.
Manageable	Represents not only what *all* students can learn but also what any *one* student can be expected to learn.

Source: The Center for Curriculum Renewal, 1998

however, conventional curriculum approaches rarely spell out assumptions about good practice. When good practice is articulated, it describes specific disciplines, not the program as a whole.

Educators now have access to a significant body of research about effective education practice. Even when viewed through different philosophies or perspectives, this research provides sound guidance. Professional development alone will not lead to consistent good practice throughout a school or district. Instead, schools and districts must articulate a set of instructional guidelines to which all teachers can refer as they plan instruction.

A state-level set of instructional guidelines was adopted as part of the *Vermont Framework of Standards and Learning Opportunities*. Figure 1.3 shows the major areas of curriculum, instruction, and assessment addressed by this document.

FIGURE 1.3

Questions Addressed in Instructional Guidelines

These are five key areas in developing instructional guidelines for standards linking; a focusing question for each area is provided.

Area	Questions
Access	To what resources (staff, material, facilities) must students have access if they are to attain the identified standards?
Instruction	What instructional approaches are most effective in supporting student learning in relation to standards?
Assessment	How is standards-based learning best measured and documented?
Connections	What connections within and across classrooms and the community need to be made in order to realize the district's vision for student learning?
Best Practices in the Discipline	Which of the content-specific instructional approaches particular to each of the disciplines are essential to implement?
The Center for Curriculum Renewal, 1998	

Clear articulation of districtwide expectations in the area of curriculum, instruction, and assessment leads to much greater consistency across classrooms. Clear articulation provides guidance for teacher decision making and establishes a common language and focus for several important areas: professional and school development, supervision and evaluation, and planning for comprehensive assessment systems and action planning.

Professional and School Development

Several resources do a fine job of defining criteria for high-quality professional development. *Continuing to Learn: A Guidebook for Professional Development* (The Regional Lab of the Northeast and Islands, 1987) broke new ground by bringing to the forefront a variety of delivery models beyond courses and workshops. A more recent publication is *Designing Professional Development for Teachers of Science and Mathematics* (Loucks-Horsley, Hewson, Love, & Styles, 1998). This book expands on those models and provides criteria and examples of programs specific to math and science. The National Staff Development Council also has developed standards for professional development.

Despite an abundance of resources, few districts have adapted the kind of long-term, data-informed systems of school and professional development needed to support all students' attainment of standards. For example, some effective professional development experiences are driven by a well-defined image of effective classroom learning and teaching.

• Provide opportunities for teachers to build their knowledge and skills.
• Use or model with teachers the strategies teachers will use

with their students.

- Build a learning community.
- Support teachers to serve in leadership roles.
- Provide links to other parts of the education system.
- Are continuously being assessed and improved by developers and presenters to ensure positive impact on teacher effectiveness, student learning, leadership, and the school community (Loucks-Horsley et al., 1998, pp. 36–37)

School and professional development within the standards linking system is needs-driven, long-term, and directly linked to the district's vision, curriculum and assessment plan, and instructional guidelines. A two- to four-year plan based on the following questions will lead to coherent school and staff development in support of standards. (Professional development is discussed in detail in Chapter 7.)

Evaluation and Needs Assessment

- What do teachers and administrators need to better teach and assess our identified standards?
- On what strengths can we draw?
- What are our priorities for professional development?
- What activities will meet the greatest needs?
- Who decides what the plan will be?
- What process will be used to develop the plan?
- How can our plan best respond to theories of adult learning?
- How can we incorporate a range of experiences from informal to formal?
- Which activities need to be individual? Small group? Whole school? System wide?

• What time frame does the plan cover? Is that the right duration?

• Where will we get the expertise needed to support the plan? From inside the system? From outside the system? People? Books? Journals? Processes? Other?

• Through what roles will colleagues support one another in the learning process? Participant? Mentor? Peer coach? Team member? Study group member? Advisory council member? Committee member?

• Who is responsible for what?

• What actions steps need to be taken?

• What is the time line for the action steps?

• What modifications are needed?

Supervision and Evaluation

In the standards-linking system, supervision and evaluation have a single focus: improved student performance. The focus is realized through three components: goal setting and formative evaluation, colleague consultation and support, and administrative evaluation and support and summative evaluation.

Goal setting is an evaluation process by which a teacher sets professional goals, alone or in conjunction with a colleague, mentor, or supervisor. The emphasis is on personal responsibility for professional growth. The teacher sets goals and assesses personal progress in relation to those goals. The colleague, mentor, or supervisor provides support, resources, and feedback.

Colleague consultation is a process by which a colleague provides support, direction, and feedback to a peer in a nonevaluative context. Colleague consultation is often used to support teachers new to a school or district or to teaching (mentoring), by veteran teachers to support one another in exploring new directions (study groups, committees, advisory groups), or by veteran teachers to support one another in pursuing new directions (peer coaching). The colleague consultants are assigned or selected, and agreement is reached on the focus of the consultation. The teacher performs self-assessments and documents progress, and discusses this information with a colleague who provides feedback and direction. The process may involve classroom observation, conferences, review of student work, or development of a professional portfolio (see Chapter 7 for more information on colleague consultants.)

In administrative evaluation and support, an administrator provides judgments and feedback related to teacher performance. These judgments may be tied to decisions of continued employment and other high-stakes decisions, such as promotion or merit pay. The emphasis is on making high-stakes decisions. The process involves a preconference, observation, written summative assessment, and a postconference.

The three processes described here are reminiscent of clinical supervision. They are necessary aspects of supervision and evaluation in the standards-linking system. To be complete, however, the system must incorporate an explicit focus on student learning as defined by the district's standards. Following are some critical questions (which are explored further in Chapter 7):

• How are the identified standards used in determining the focus for supervision and evaluation?
  • What does the standards-based classroom look like?
  • How are the standards used in self-assessment?
  • How are the standards used in goal setting?
  • How are the standards used in colleague consultation?
  • How are the standards used in summative evaluation?

The Comprehensive Assessment System

Standards bring focus and purpose to the design of comprehensive assessment systems at state, local, and classroom levels. Historically, school districts have focused on input: the money and materials provided to support student learning. In response to standards, the first tendency is to switch to a focus on student results. Instead, schools need a balanced approach, a truly comprehensive system that includes state, local, and classroom components *and* includes data about inputs (resources), processes (programs and practices), and outputs (student results).

A comprehensive assessment plan is a written document that spells out the district's plan to assess progress toward implementing and meeting the standards. The plan should

• Enhance and not unnecessarily distract from student learning.

• Include state, district, and classroom components.

• Clearly identify at which of those three levels each of the standards will be assessed.

• Match the types of assessment used to the demands of the standard assessed.

• Require that assessment results are reported to students, educators, parents, community members, and policymakers.

• Specifically identify how the data will be used.

• Provide information necessary for public accountability and reporting.

• Be balanced in terms of time, resources, and capacity required.

Once the comprehensive assessment plan has been compiled, the comprehensive assessment system really puts the plan into action.

The comprehensive assessment system

• Enables the school or district to implement the local comprehensive assessment plan.
• Provides quality control for technical issues.
• Provides quality control for ethical issues.
• Links to action planning and ensures that data is actually used for student, school, and program improvement.
• Includes policy and leadership support needed to implement the local comprehensive assessment plan.
• Includes professional development and a support system for those implementing the program.
• Includes procedures to evaluate and revise the local comprehensive assessment plan and system.

Chapter 4 provides information and examples of local comprehensive assessment plans and systems.

Action Plans

Ultimately, results from a standards-linking system occur because of the link between the vision, the comprehensive assessment plan, and a concrete, operational action plan for systemwide improvement. An action plan is distinguished from the more common organizational strategic plan by its direct and explicit focus on improvement of student learning. Action planning is the focus of Chapter 5. Briefly, an action plan is

• Based on data from the comprehensive assessment system, including but not limited to data on student results.
• Developed through engagement of teachers, administrators, and community members.

• Reviewed and revised yearly.

• Specific with regard to actions, responsibilities, and resources needed.

• Time limited for maximum effect.

The following chapters provide information, examples, and tools for getting started in the process of bringing standards to life in schools and districts. Remember that this is not a linear process. In fact, you may discover it makes sense to start in several places at once, working on the beginnings of a professional development plan at the same time that the status of standards is being determined or creating instructional guidelines while the comprehensive assessment system is being created. Helping all students attain standards is not a matter of business as usual. It is an ongoing process of questioning our own assumptions, acknowledging the best of past practice, and creating new and better ways to proceed.

2

The Curriculum
and Assessment Plan

Adopting standards is a necessary step toward improving student learning. But the work put into creating a standards document will have little long-term effect without definite decisions about who teaches and assesses standards and when. Although the decisions seem simple and straightforward, few schools and districts take their standards and create explicit plans for how to implement those standards in the classroom.

Strengths and Limitations
of Scope-and-Sequence Documents

Historically, the design of local curriculum has been synonymous with the publication of scope-and-sequence documents for various subject areas. These documents show a progression of content and skills for grades K–12. Sometimes the content and skills are spelled out in minute detail; at other times they are described in general terms. Sometimes the scope-and-sequence documents reflect materials being used; at other times, curriculum committees develop scope-and-sequence documents based on research and best practice.

The process of developing a scope-and-sequence document engages those involved in important conversations about critical content and skills. Shared understandings and commitments evolve from these conversations. Other advantages of a scope-and-sequence document are that content and skills are broken down in logical progressions and the documents make public what is to be taught and learned in the school or district.

Unfortunately, we have found several disadvantages to the scope-and-sequence approach, particularly in a standards-based environment:

• Not all schools and districts have the content or curriculum expertise in all subject areas to enable them to develop accurate, high-quality scope-and-sequence documents.

• When the contents of the scope-and-sequence documents are added together, the materials are often more than even the most capable students could possibly learn in grades K–12. Thus, teachers discount the scope-and-sequence documents, and they use materials inconsistently.

• Scope-and-sequence documents are often developed by different committees of teachers, therefore they use different formats and language. Therefore, the documents are difficult to use with one another, which is a key challenge for elementary teachers who are responsible for teaching all subject areas.

• Scope-and-sequence documents typically lack an explicit link to student performance. Therefore, curriculum accountability addresses what is "covered," not what is learned.

• Scope-and-sequence documents usually give little guidance for instruction or assessment.

Once they adopt standards, many schools and districts revise existing scope-and-sequence documents to show which content and skills relate to which standards. This approach makes an explicit commitment to standards, but this work is not enough for planning standards-based learning. Too often the connections are weak or insufficient, consequently some standards get left out or the overall picture of standards implementation remains unclear. Revising a scope-and-sequence document describes how standards fit into the existing curriculum documents, but does not answer how to best support students as they seek to attain standards.

Standards: A Powerful Alternative

Standards are public and shared across schools and districts. Standards encompass accurate, high-quality content and skills. Standards are a balanced, coherent articulation of expectations for student learning. Standards provide the structure from which a deep and rich local curriculum can be built.

When standards replace scope-and-sequence documents, the local curriculum reflects

• Decisions about the standards, at which grade levels they will be taught and assessed, and how often.

• Student assessment profiles showing which information about student learning will be recorded and kept over time.

• Instructional guidelines articulating the school's or district's commitment to approaches designed to support student learning in relation to the identified standards.

• A resource bank of high-quality standards-based classroom assessments, units of study, and published materials that can be shared and used across classrooms and schools.

Who Is Responsible for What?

Decisions about where the standards will be taught and assessed are at the heart of a curriculum and assessment plan. How often will the standards be taught? At what grade levels? In what courses? Cross-grade committees, grade-level teams, high school departments, and other groups can make preliminary decisions in these areas using a database of information about who teaches and assesses which standards (see Chapter 1). Groups also can start with recommendations from representative teachers about what *should* be taught and assessed at what points throughout the system. Once a draft is created, the whole faculty needs to review the plan. Are the standards appropriately placed? Are there any undesirable gaps or overlaps? Are there issues that need to be addressed? Figure 2.1 (pp. 21–22) shows a page from the decisions made by one district.

In our experience, individual schools often expand work done at the district level. For example, many high schools soon realize that the standards they are assigned to teach are not taught and assessed for all students in their current delivery system. At one small rural high school, members of the science department discovered that all of the standards assigned to science in the curriculum and assessment plan were, in fact, taught in the existing physics course. The problem was that only eight students took that course each year.

Sometimes it is easier to track an issue by comparing the curriculum and assessment plan with the standards that are already taught and assessed in each course within a department. Figure 2.2 (pp. 23–24) shows the status of standards taught in various science courses in one high school.

Similarly, elementary and middle schools need to take the district curriculum and assessment plan and identify the themes and topics that will be used in the school for teaching and assessing standards. It is important to track these themes and topics directly against the district document, however, or standards easily get lost in the process.

FIGURE 2.1

Curriculum and Assessment Plan Example

This is part of a curriculum and assessment plan developed using standards linking. The plan indicates what standards and evidence will be taught and assessed in each of four academic disciplines.

X = Skills should be taught and assessed

A = Skills should be assessed in this subject area

I = Skills should be instructed in this subject area

STD = Standards

WSWSU Draft Curriculum #2 8/29/99			Science		Math		English		Social Studies							
			I	A	I	A	I	A	I	A	I	A	I	A	I	A
COMMUNICATION																
1.1	Std	Reading Strategies — Students use a variety of strategies to help them read. This is evident when students use a combination of strategies including:	X	X	X	X	X	X	X	X							
1.1a	K–4	Sounds, syllables, and letter patterns (e.g., phonological, phonic, and graphic knowledge)					X	X									
1.1b	K–4	Syntax					X	X									
1.1c	K–4	Meaning in context					X	X									
1.1d	K–4	A range of cueing systems to discover pronunciation and meaning					X	X									
1.1e	K–4	Self-correcting when subsequent reading indicates an earlier miscue					X	X									

FIGURE 2.1—continued

Curriculum and Assessment Plan Example

WSWSU Draft Curriculum #2 8/29/99			Science		Math		English		Social Studies							
			I	A	I	A	I	A	I	A	I	A	I	A	I	A
COMMUNICATION																
1.1f	K–4	Questioning					X	X								
1.1g	K–4	Prior knowledge of the topic and sense of story					X	X								
1.1h	5–8	Predicting					X	X	X	X						
1.1i	5–8	Skimming					X	X								
1.1j	5–8	Following themes					X	X	X	X						
1.1k	5–8	Previewing for book selection (e.g., for content, form, style)	X		X	X	X	X	X	X						

Source: Windsor Southwest Supervisory Union (Chester, VT) and the Center for Curriculum Renewal.

FIGURE 2.2

High School Science Example

The table shows the science classes (listed across the top) offered at a high school, as compared with the topics of the standards (listed down the side). A similar process is used in each academic area to determine which standards are covered in each class.

Science Class / Standard	Physical Science	Earth Science	Biology	Chemistry	Science and Technology	AP Biology	Advanced Biology	Physics
7.1	7.1cc	7.1cc	7.1cc	7.1cc 7.1ii	7.1aaa 7.1bbb 7.1ddd 7.1ggg 7.1hh	7.1aaa 7.1bbb 7.1ddd	7.1aaa 7.1bbb 7.1ggg	7.1aaa 7.1bbb 7.1ddd
7.2	7.2aa	7.2aa	7.2aa	7.2aa	7.2aa	7.2aa	7.2aa	7.2aa
7.3			7.3aa	7.3aa	7.3aaa			
7.4	7.4aa	7.4aa	7.4aa	7.4aa		7.4aa	7.4aa	7.4aa
7.5	7.5aa	7.5aa	7.5aa	7.5 aa	7.5aaa	7.5aa	7.5aaa	
7.11				7.11aaa 7.11cc	7.11aaa 7.11bbb			
7.12	7.12ddd 7.12dd 7.12eee			7.12aaa 7.12bbb 7.12ccc 7.12eee	7.12aaa 7.12bbb 7.12ddd 7.12fff			7.12ddd 7.12eee 7.12fff
7.13			7.13aaa 7.13bbb 7.13ccc 7.13ddd 7.15eee		7.13ccc	7.13aaa 7.13bbb 7.13ccc 7.13ddd	7.13aaa 7.13bbb 7.13ccc	

FIGURE 2.2—continued

High School Science Example

Science Class / Standard	Physical Science	Earth Science	Biology	Chemistry	Science and Technology	AP Biology	Advanced Biology	Physics
7.14						7.14aaa 7.14bbb 7.14ddd	7.14aaa 7.14bbb 7.14ccc 7.14ddd	
7.15		7.15aaa 7.15bbb 7.15ccc 7.15dd			7.15eee		7.15eee	7.15ddd
7.16				7.16bbb 7.16ccc 7.16dd	7.16aaa 7.16bbb			
7.17					7.17aaa 7.17ddd			
7.18				7.18aaa	7.18aaa 7.18bbb 7.18ddd			
7.19					7.19aaa 7.19bbb			7.19aaa 7.19bbb

Courtesy of Brian O'Regan, Superintendent, Chittenden South Supervisory Union

Standards and Spiraling

The fundamental decision in developing standards-based curriculum is assigning standards to specific grade levels, courses, or classroom settings. However, repeating standards also involves careful decision-making. Two common complaints about curriculum in the United States relate to repetition. In some subject areas, such as science and social studies, the curriculum is described as "a mile wide and an inch deep." And the fact that U.S. 4th graders perform well in international comparisons, while 8th and 10th graders do less well, is partially attributed to repetition at the same level of complexity, rather than moving to complex content and concepts (Third International Mathematics and Science Study, 1998).

Standards are frequently written in grade-level clusters (such as K–4, 5–8, and 9–12), therefore educators must decide which standards should be repeated at specific grade levels and in certain courses. One of the most effective ways to repeat standards is through a spiral curriculum. In a standards-based spiral curriculum, students return to certain standards and evidence at prescribed intervals. However, the standards are taught and learned at a higher level of complexity with each repetition. There are three ways to increase the complexity of standards and evidence:

- Increase the complexity of the content.
- Increase the complexity of how students interact with the content.
- Increase both the complexity of student interaction with the content and the complexity of the content itself.

Here is a standard and one example of accompanying evidence from *Vermont's Framework of Standards and Learning Opportunities*.

Standard 1.13: Students respond to literary texts and public documents using interpretive, critical, and evaluation processes. This is evident when students:

a. Make inferences about content, events, story, characters, and setting, and about the relationship(s) among them.

This standard and evidence applies to all grades, K–12.

The complexity of the content evolves as the student matures. With the standard cited above, the student may begin with picture books, move to chapter books, biography, and textbooks, and continue with primary sources and complex scientific treatises.

The curriculum can also increase the complexity of how the student interacts with the content. A young student might begin at enumeration, listing events, character, and setting. As she matures, she might identify relationships among the elements listed in the evidence. Later, she might make inferences based on these relationships, develop hypotheses, and verify predictions through extended research.

Unlike the previous example, all standards and evidence do not remain constant over the K–12 spectrum. Figure 2.3 shows an example of how the *Georgia Framework for Learning Mathematics and Science* spirals the concept of number systems.

Everyday Mathematics, developed by the University of Chicago School Mathematics Project, introduces negative numbers, fractions, decimals, and percents at the primary level. However, "prior to fourth grade, negative numbers, fractions, decimals, and percents were used mainly to convey information, without becoming involved in operations such as addition, subtraction, and division" (University of Chicago School Mathematics Project, 1995). This is an example of spiraling complexity of application of content; in Georgia schools implementing *Everyday Math*, the content is introduced prior to students' responsibility to perform in relation to the standard. Figure 2.4 contains questions that may be used in making decisions related to spiraling.

FIGURE 2.3

Spiraling Concept Sample

A concept may spiral through the curriculum, increasing in depth and complexity, as students mature and gain experience and expertise in the content. The following example of a spiraling concept is for mathematics and shows how students learn about the number system.

Primary: Understand the numeration system by relating counting, grouping, and place value.
Elementary: Extend the number system to include fractions, decimals, and integers.
Middle Grades: Extend the development of the number system through the use of integers.
High School: Compare and contrast the real number systems and its various subsystems with regard to their structural characteristics.

Adapted from Georgia Initiative on Math and Science, 1997

The answers to the questions in Figure 2.4 should guide you in determining what standards and evidence to spiral. They should also help to address the two criticisms discussed at the beginning of this section: By returning to fundamental standards it is possible to limit the scope of the curriculum and to increase its depth, thus building a richer, focused curriculum.

The Student Assessment Profile

The K–12 Student Assessment Profile is a compilation of assessment information for each student. The profile contains a selection of assessments that highlight and track student performance and progress over time toward meeting standards. The profile

FIGURE 2.4

Sample Spiraling Questions

The following questions may help curriculum developers to build spiraling into standards linking.

Which standards and evidence will be spiraled in the standards-based curriculum?

The general rule of thumb is that each standard and evidence will be experienced at least once per grade level cluster. Typically, this commitment will consume the most teaching and learning time. Selection of standards for spiraling should be confined to those that are at the foundation of the disciplines, such as inquiry for science or map skills for social studies, and to those cutting across disciplines, such as communication, problem solving, and personal development. Rarely is there time or justification for spiraling specific content areas, such as dinosaurs or the Civil War within a grade level cluster; however, these may well be revisited across clusters.

How will students experience the standards and evidence at each level?

The purpose of spiraling is to increase the complexity of content and of the application of that content over time. Make sure that the repetition of the standard and evidence isn't more of the same, at the same level of complexity. Pay attention to developmental progression. For example, how might a 5th grader and an 8th grader differ in their approach to civic and social responsibility? Given this developmental progression, what experiences might be provided at each grade level?

What ways will students apply the standard at each level?

As each of the examples above illustrated, returning to a standard generally implies a different level of application of principles. How will students use what they have learned? Is this substantively different from the first experience?

What ways will the student critically examine the standard at each level?

Finally, are there fundamental differences in how the student can examine the standards and evidence upon returning to them? Can they make finer distinctions between similarities and differences? Can they predict consequences or explain phenomena at a different level?

Center for Curriculum Renewal

paints a picture of student performance, and it complements the decisions made about classroom assessments that are shown in the curriculum and assessment plan. The Student Assessment Profile is NOT the results of all, or even of most, assessments in which a student takes part in the classroom. Instead, the profile is a manageable, efficient, small sampling of assessment information about each student, captured over time. The Student Assessment Profile

- Informs parents, teachers and students of student progress toward meeting selected standards.
- Includes selected assessments that measure chosen standards across the grades from K–12 in a balanced distribution by grade and content.
- Can be used to look at the effectiveness of programs over time, as well as to look at student progress toward meeting standards.
- Assesses standards that are representative of the whole set of standards, and of all grade levels.

We worked with one district that engaged a cross-grade-level committee of teachers and administrators in five day-long meetings to create their student assessment profile. The following information describes what the committee accomplished in each session. You may be able to adapt this to the work in your school.

Session 1
- Developed a common understanding of a student assessment profile.
- Shared existing assessments currently used in the district.
- Identified standards to include in the profile.

Session 2
- Completed initial identification of standards for the student assessment profile.

OUACHITA TECHNICAL COLLEGE

• Reviewed potential assessments, which assess standards we identified.

Session 3

• Prioritized which standards will be assessed and when and where they will be assessed for grades K–12.

    • Completed a first draft of the Student Assessment Profile.

    • Determined a process for gathering feedback from colleagues.

Session 4

    • Reviewed feedback from colleagues.

    • Revised the student assessment profile to be more realistic.

    • Refined the comprehensive assessment plan (See Chapter 4) by incorporating decisions made about the student assessment profile, considering whether other information is needed about student results, and making decisions about what data to collect about available resources and the actual implementation of programs and practices.

Session 5

    • Finalized the student assessment profile.

    • Generated recommendations for phasing in the student assessment profile and identifying professional development needs.

    • Identified implementation needs specific to each school.

The committee's first draft of standards and possible assessments was lengthy, but the list gave them a place to start considering what would work best. Possible assessments were drawn from a Web site developed using Goals 2000 Funds by the Vermont Standards and Assessment Consortium (http://www.dbweb.ed.state.vt.us/arb). Other suggestions came from committee members. Existing state assessments were included as well (see Figure 2.5).

OUACHITA TECHNICAL COLLEGE

FIGURE 2.5

Student Assessment Profile

The following table shows the decisions made by a school district in developing a student assessment profile through standards linking. These decisions were related to one standard (reading accuracy) across all grade levels, K–12. Similar decisions are made for other standards and evidence.

Potential Standards to Include in Profile	Possible Assessments	Other Assessments/Comments
Communication 1.2 (Reading Accuracy) Students read grade-appropriate material, with 90%+ accuracy, in a way that makes meaning clear.	**Language Arts** • Oral Reading Fluency Scoring Guide—3rd Grade • Grade 2 Vermont Developmental Reading Assessment • Primary and 2–4 Literacy/Communication Profiles by Biggam, Herman, and Trubisz • K–4 Texas Primary Reading Inventory • K–12 Information Literacy Rubrics **Multiple Subjects** • K–12 The Litter Challenge • 5–8 Williston Student Engagement Rubrics • K–12 Communication of Data **Science** • 9–12 Golden State Exam Science Portfolio **Social Studies** • 5–8; 9–12 Vermont History Projects • K–12 Riverside Performance Assessment Series	

Source: Windsor Southwest Supervisory Union and the Center for Curriculum Renewal

The committee then used an assessment checklist adopted by the Vermont Standards and Assessment Consortium to select only the highest quality assessments to include in the student assessment profile (see Figure 2.6, pp. 34–35). This checklist was adapted from Joan Herman's "Technical Quality Matters" (1996). The checklist is intended to provide a profile of an assessment tool in relation to identified standards. A single "No Response" would not, in most cases, remove a tool from consideration.

In the end, the committee divided the profile into grade-level blocks: K–2, 3–4, 5–6, and 7–12. They created forms for each grade-level block for tracking assessment information for each student. At the time of this writing, the district is in the process of converting these forms to online templates to simplify record keeping, to save time, and to provide easier access for appropriate educational personnel. Figure 2.7 (pp. 36–37) shows an excerpt from the Grades 3–4 profile focused on literacy standards.

In creating your own student assessment profile, consider the following questions:

- Are the assessed standards representative of the whole set of standards?
- Is the number of standards included a reasonable number?
- Are the assessments of high quality?
- What will be the impact of these assessments on the students who participate in them?
- Will the information provided be useful feedback to students and parents?
- Will the information provided be useful in instructional planning and program improvement?
- Does the profile, as a whole, accurately reflect student performance over time?

FIGURE 2.6

Assessment Checklist

This checklist can be used to develop a profile of an assessment considered for use in the student assessment profile. The checklist may also be used in developing a comprehensive assessment plan.

Consequences
❑ Is the assessment worth the instructional time?
❑ Does the assessment encourage good instruction as defined by the district's instructional guidelines?
❑ Does the assessment support a curricular focus related to the standards and instructional guidelines?

Fairness
❑ Does the assessment provide exemplars appropriate to the level for which it is designed?
❑ Does the assessment provide ample time for students to finish so that results reflect capability rather than test-taking skill?
❑ Does the assessment tap the knowledge and skills students have had an adequate opportunity to acquire during classroom instruction?
❑ Is the assessment free of cultural, ethnic, and gender stereotype?
❑ Is the assessment free of tasks or situations more familiar to students of one background or gender than another?
❑ Does the assessment use a scoring process applied without bias?
❑ Does the assessment avoid unnecessarily difficult language when assessing content from the standards?
❑ Does the assessment enable all students to demonstrate what they know and can do in the areas being assessed?
❑ Can necessary accommodations be used?

Reliability and Validity
❑ Does the assessment describe the standards it intends to assess?
❑ Does the assessment represent the intended standards?
❑ Does the assessment provide evidence that the results are generalizable—are indicative of student performance in a broader domain of knowledge?
❑ Does the assessment design include consideration of the number of tasks a student must complete in order to yield generalizable results?
❑ Does the assessment include explicit criteria for scoring and preferably a guide describing the application of these criteria?
❑ Does the assessment provide evidence that results are consistent across raters and across scoring occasions?

FIGURE 2.6—continued

Assessment Checklist

Cognitive Complexity
❑ Does the assessment use tasks for which students can be expected to have adequate background knowledge?
❑ Does the assessment use tasks whose solutions cannot be memorized in advance?
❑ Does the assessment assess key concepts and principles from the standards?
❑ Does the assessment provide evidence that tasks elicit complex understanding or problem-solving skills?

Content Quality and Coverage
❑ Does the assessment use tasks consistent with the instructional guidelines?
❑ Has the assessment been reviewed by content experts to ensure quality, accuracy, and disciplinary and interdisciplinary appropriateness of tasks?
❑ Does the assessment format reflect classroom practice?

Meaningfulness
❑ Does the assessment provide useful information for students, parents, and teachers?
❑ Is the assessment credible to teachers, students, parents, and the public as a valid indicator of student competence in the particular assessment area?
❑ Does the assessment engage and motivate students to do their best?

Cost and Efficiency
❑ Is the assessment administratively feasible?
❑ Is the assessment cost-efficient?

Adapted from the work of Joan Herman; permission from The Vermont Standards and Assessment Consortium and the Center for Curriculum Renewal

Implications for the Classroom

In the process of developing the curriculum and assessment plan and the student assessment profile, questions frequently arise about classroom assessment. What does it mean to say we will assess this standard at this grade level? Are we using the right sort of assessments? How do we create assessments to align with standards?

Classroom assessment is much more than tests, rubrics, and giving grades. Assessment is an integral part of instruction. Assessment is the process of quantifying, describing, gathering data about, or giving feedback about performance. The primary purpose of standards-based classroom assessment is to inform teaching and improve learning. In addition, assessment

- Guides the process of changing and improving education.
- Determines the success of individual students, specific curricula, and institutional practice.
- Determines if students have integrated knowledge and skills across the curricula.
- Provides methods and data to effectively communicate results.

Effective classroom assessments are ongoing and relevant to immediate learning, as well as

- Comprehensive
    - Each component is part of a whole system.
    - Addresses needs of a variety of audiences.
    - Addresses student strengths as well as problems.
    - Examines results within and across curricula.
- Inclusive
    - Multifaceted and flexible.
    - Developmentally and culturally appropriate.
    - Addresses learning styles and multiple intelligences.
    - Involves the student in self-assessment.
- Technically Sound
    - Continuous and ongoing.
    - Valid and reliable.
    - Reported accurately.

FIGURE 2.7

Grades 3–4 Profile Example

This is an example of page from a student assessment profile. The word "score" is a placeholder for actual student scores. In some instances, student performance sheets are attached to the profile. A gray block indicates that the assessment is not used at the time and grade level indicated.

Third and Fourth Grade Language Arts Student Assessment Profile

Assessment	Vermont Standard	Grade 3 Fall	Grade 3 Winter	Grade 3 Spring	Grade 4 Fall	Grade 4 Winter	Grade 4 Spring
Informal Reading Inventory Word recognition Using Burns and Roe	1.1 1.2 1.3	score	score		score	score	
Informal Reading Inventory Comprehension Using Burns and Roe	1.1 1.2 1.3	score	score	score	score	score	
Achievement Test	Cross-check when new test is selected			score			
New Standard Exam English and Language Arts	1.3 1.7						Attach student sheet

FIGURE 2.7—continued

Grades 3–4 Profile Example

Third and Fourth Grade Language Arts Student Assessment Profile

Assessment	Vermont Standard	Grade 3 Fall	Grade 3 Winter	Grade 3 Spring	Grade 4 Fall	Grade 4 Winter	Grade 4 Spring
Genre Tracking Sheet (Database is on computer—print and attach completed form)	5.8 5.9 1.4			Attach sheet			Attach sheet
Spelling Assessment	1.6	score		score	score		score
Writing Prompt (Score using rubrics for narratives and conventions)	1.5 1.6						
Writing Portfolio	1.8 1.9 1.10 1.11		Narrative Score:	Responses to Literature Score:		Procedures Score:	Reports Score:

Source: Windsor Southwest Supervisory Union and the Center for Curriculum Renewal

When planning for assessment, consider the bigger picture. This means developing an assessment plan. An assessment plan is a design tool, a set of choices regarding how student learning will be assessed in relation to standards, and its use ensures that

• The feedback from implementation of an assessment plan guides the process of changing and improving instruction.

• There will be multiple opportunities for a student to demonstrate attainment of an identified standard.

• Students will produce a variety of constructed responses, such as products (written reports, diorama, map) and performances (orienteering course, interview, play). Variety of responses recognizes multiple intelligences and individual student strengths. Selected responses and short answer assessments are often also part of the plan.

• A variety of scoring guides will be used to provide feedback on student learning.

Some teachers develop assessment plans unit-by-unit and for the published materials they use. Others develop more holistic plans tied to the standards for which they are responsible. The assessment plan includes information about the products and performances to be assessed, the scoring guides that will be used for feedback, the reporting and feedback methods, and who the assessors will be. Figure 2.8 shows definitions of the assessment planning guide developed by the Vermont Department of Education. Figure 2.9 shows an example of part of an assessment plan from a science unit created by Nicole Pfister, a 6th grade teacher at the Flood Brook School in Londonderry, Vermont.

How to Use Standards in the Classroom (Harris & Carr, 1996) provides additional useful information about design of scoring guides and units of study. Planning for instruction in and assessment of standards in the classroom is an important step in the process of implementing standards in a school or district. In the next chapter, we turn our attention to the question, "What opportunities to learn do students need if *all* students are to attain the standards?"

Figure 2.8

Assessment Planning Guide

This assessment planning guide can be used in action planning. The columns represent four types of assessments (selected response and three types of constructed responses). For each type of assessment, three types of information are provided: a definition, a description of the type of scoring guide used to collect student data, and the form in which results are reported to students, parents, and others.

What the Student Produces	Selected Response	Constructed Response: Short Answers	Constructed Response: Products	Constructed Response: Performances
Definition	Student selects from among responses that are presented	The student must create a response or answer	Documents or artifacts created by students	Demonstrations and interactions carried out by students
Scoring Guides	Answer key machine scoring template	Generalized or task-specific rubric checklist	Generalized or task-specific rubric checklist	Generalized or task-specific rubric checklist
Reporting or Feedback	Numerical score: percentages, total points	Numerical score: percentages, total points	Numerical score: percentages, total points	Numerical score: percentages, total points
	letter grades	letter grades	letter grades	letter grades
	narrative report (written)	narrative report (written)	narrative report (written)	narrative report (written)
	checklist	checklist	checklist	checklist
	comments	comments	comments	comments
	verbal	verbal	verbal	verbal

Source: Vermont Department of Education, 1999

FIGURE 2.9

Example of an Assessment Plan

This assessment plan was developed by a 6th grade teacher for a science unit. In this example, the teacher did not use selected response assessments. Although exams and quizzes may include selected responses, in this case the items on the exams and quizzes were all constructed response items. The plan indicates the types of scoring guides used for each assessment.

What the Student Produces	Selected Response	Constructed Response: Short Answers	Constructed Response: Products	Constructed Response: Performances
Standard 7.1		• Exam • Quiz		• Cooperative lab activities • Rubric
Standard 7.12 Matter, Motion, Forces, and Energy		• Exam	• Research project • Essay	• Cooperative lab activities
Scoring Guides		• Answer key for exam and quiz	• Rubric for research project • Rubric for essay	• Rubric for cooperative lab activities
Nicole Pfister, Flood Brook School				

 # 3

Defining Effective Practices
for Attainment of Standards

Our colleague at Goddard College, Ken Bergstrom, suggests that of the following common student complaints about school learning, only one can be remedied by standards alone.

- "It's boring."
- "What does this have to do with me?
- "It's not fun."
- "It doesn't fit the way I learn."
- "I don't know what the teacher expects."

Only the complaint about not knowing what the teacher expects can be addressed by standards alone. All of the other common student complaints can be answered only through effective practice that helps students attain the standards.

Every student needs high-quality opportunities to learn and be assessed in relation to standards. For schools and classrooms to meet that goal, teachers must understand what experiences students need to have to attain the identified standards. A thorough review of national standards documents that include recommendations for implementation, as well as a thorough review of the literature on best practices in the areas of instruction and assessment (*Vermont's Framework of Standards and Learning Opportunities*, 1996) resulted in the following list of sample instructional guidelines. As mentioned in Chapter 1, these reflect five areas pertinent to schools and classrooms: access, instruction, assessment and reporting, connections, and best practices in the fields of knowledge.

The following sample instructional guidelines can be adopted or adapted to accompany your own local curriculum and assessment plan, or they can serve as a model for developing your own set of instructional guidelines. What is important is that you have clear, public commitments to the supports students require if they are to reach the identified standards. These then become a basis for data collection and action planning (see Chapter 5) and for professional development and supervision and evaluation (see Chapter 7).

Sample Instructional Guidelines

Access

Access to Content

Students need to have access to the knowledge and skills described in the standards. Students can access the standards if the

- Local curriculum is based on the standards.
- Concepts and skills based on the standards are woven throughout the grades to provide an opportunity to develop increasing levels of sophistication and understanding over time (e.g., understanding of atomic theory built on early explorations into the physical properties of objects).
- Content is accurate and is updated as new information emerges.
- Units of study are current and coordinated within the school (e.g., across classrooms and grade levels) and beyond the school (e.g., within the supervisory union, school-to-work region).

Access to Instructors

Students need access to instructors who ar knowledgeable about the disciplines they teach, about the developmental characteristics of the students they teach, and about best practices in learning and teaching. For example, instructors demonstrate accessibility and knowledge when they

- Plan developmentally appropriate curriculum and instruction.
- Present accurate knowledge through multiple perspectives and connected disciplines (e.g., studying the Civil War from historical, economic, and literary perspectives).
- Continually update units of study to include new and revised information, current standards, and appropriate instructional strategies.

Students also need access to instructors who share their knowledge, who work with others to plan and assess curriculum, and who themselves are continually learning. For example, instructors demonstrate this principle when they

- Participate in a variety of professional development experiences to increase their knowledge of content and learning and teaching (e.g., coaching, study groups, collaborative curriculum development, business internship, independent study).
- Work with others (e.g., colleagues, parents, content area experts, other community members, and students) to plan and assess curriculum.

Access to Resources

Students need equitable and prompt access to accurate materials and current resources (in addition to textbooks) that are appropriate for learning goals. For example, students need

• Frequent opportunities to engage the community as a resource and a learning laboratory (e.g., learning from artists, businesses, health-care providers, town records, town meetings, community theater, the local landfill).

• Access to a variety of information-technology tools (e.g., libraries, computers, telecommunications).

• Access to all services provided within the school (e.g., guidance services, technical education, special education, speech and language support, health services, enrichment).

• Access to resource materials that are free of bias, stereotyping, and misrepresentation.

• Access to facilities and equipment necessary to support the instructional process.

Access to Time

Students need instruction that uses time effectively and flexibly to achieve learning goals. Evidence of instruction that demonstrates flexibility and efficient use of time occurs when

• Schedules are built around learning and instructional needs (e.g., flexible blocks).

• Teachers give input on external events or intrusions (e.g., timing of announcements, schedules, and special events) that have an effect on the day.

• Noninstructional time is used in creative and purposeful ways (e.g., taking lunch count in Spanish).

• Time is built in for collaboration (e.g., student with teacher, teacher with teacher, teacher with family).

• Maximum time is devoted to student "time on task," with high levels of student engagement in constructive learning tasks.

Access to a Safe and Healthy Environment

Students need to learn in an environment that is physically and emotionally safe and educationally supportive. The following examples are indicative of safe environments.

- Equipment, work, and learning spaces are maintained and organized so that tasks and projects may be carried out safely.
- Adults are healthy and model healthy behaviors (e.g., a smoke-free, drug-free environment).
- Each student has access to a caring adult.
- Policies and rules are fair, known to all, and consistently applied.

Instruction

Acquiring Knowledge and Skills

Students need learning experiences that engage them in active learning, build on prior knowledge and experiences, and develop conceptual and procedural understanding, along with student independence.

- Begin learning experiences by setting a context or previewing possible applications.
- Use strategies that help students link new learning to previous knowledge and experiences (e.g., discussion of previous experiences, free writes, pretests, think-pair-share, three-minute pauses).
- Scaffold learning so that students can gradually gain expertise (e.g., removing cues over time as students learn to converse in a second language).
- Prompt students to support their statements with evidence (e.g., while comparing, classifying, constructing support for positions).

- Use strategies that help students organize and interpret new learning (e.g., have students create graphs and charts, graphic representations, flow charts, distributed practice sessions).
- Use questions that extend and refine learning (e.g., open-ended questions, error-analysis questions).
- Provide opportunities for students to bring up and explore their own misconceptions and to replace these with accurate conceptions of knowledge.

Variety of Instructor Roles

Teachers use a variety of teaching roles (e.g., direct instruction, facilitating, modeling, coaching, reflecting, guiding, observing), and adapt these as appropriate for different purposes of instruction and student needs. For example, a teacher can

- Act as explorer and colearner.
- Adopt a role determined by the purpose of the learning and the needs of the students.
- Collaborate in designing, implementing, and evaluating units of study.

Multiple Student Roles

Students need opportunities to learn through a variety of roles (e.g., planner, questioner, artist, scientist, historian) and to learn alone and with others. For example, students can

- Collaborate in both small and large groups.
- Teach other students, formally and informally.
- Pursue individual concerns, learning interests, and projects.
- Codesign (e.g., with teachers, peers) learning activities.
- Participate in opportunities available for independent learning, work in pairs, and work in larger groups.
- Have opportunities to work with professionals in the field.

Application and Reflection

Projects and assignments require students to integrate and apply their learning in meaningful contexts and to reflect on what they have learned. For example, students

- Participate in extended investigations through which they address essential questions.
  - Transfer learning from one format or context to another.
  - Design products, services, and systems.
  - Plan activities and carry out projects that meet real needs.
  - Use in-depth applications (e.g., critiques, author studies).
  - Perform reflection through a variety of modes (e.g., writing, talking, dancing, painting).

Adaptive Learning Environments

Learning environments are adapted so that all students achieve success. These environments allow

- Appropriate instructional strategies to be selected based on what is known from learning theory (e.g., multiple intelligences, learning styles, language development).
  - Teachers to assess students' needs and use that information to form groups and to modify and adapt instruction.
  - Stakeholders involved with the child's learning experience (e.g., family members, teachers, health-care providers, business partners, bus drivers) opportunities to collaborate to meet student needs.
  - Standards to be the framework for learning; time, strategies, and approaches to be the variables, based on individual differences, strengths, and needs.

Assessment and Reporting

Multiple Assessment Strategies

A balance and variety of assessment strategies are used to gain information and provide feedback about student learning (e.g., performance assessments, self-assessments, paper-and-pencil tests, checklists). For example, appropriate tools and techniques are used for assessing different skills and concepts (e.g., anecdotal notes during observation of a discussion; a standards-based rubric used during a culminating project; conventional tests).

Criteria for Assessment

Expectations and performance criteria are clear and public. For example, criteria must

- Clearly define student products or performances and judge with observable criteria based on standards.
- Be publicly displayed, ideally with student work samples on walls, bookmarks, and in newsletters.

Assessment that Informs Instruction and Guides Student Learning

Assessment results are used to influence instructional decisions and to plan students' next learning steps:

- Classroom-based assessments are embedded into instruction (e.g., assessment of prior knowledge about a topic, entries in learning logs).
- Ongoing adjustment of instruction and the classroom environment is based on assessment (e.g., adding learning-teaching activities, selecting different materials, restructuring learning groups).
- Tools such as performance checklists, scales, tests, and quizzes are used appropriately before, during, and after units of study.

• Key players collaborate in assessment, gathering information from students, parents, other teachers, or community members to help build a more complete picture of student growth and achievement.

• Students participate, as appropriate, in the development of performance descriptions.

Student Involvement in Assessment

Students use clear criteria and examples to evaluate their own work. For example, students participate in

• Peer conferencing and self-reflection activities that use identified criteria (e.g., students setting criteria for assessment or using rubrics to assess cooperative group activities).

• Setting and monitoring progress toward learning goals.

Effectively Communicating Assessment Information

Classroom-based assessments are combined with other measures to communicate information about student learning. To effectively communicate critical information,

• Assessments are summarized in relation to standards.

• Results are shared with and reported to students, parents, and other professionals.

• Student achievement is compared with standards, demonstrating student growth over time and public accountability.

• Assessments must be fair, valid, and consistent (reliable).

• Report cards reflect student progress toward the standards over time, as well as student achievement of the standards.

• Students are involved in parent conferences (e.g., reviewing the quality of work and setting goals).

• Regular evaluations are conducted to determine how effectively assessments are being communicated (e.g., interviews with students, a survey of parent responses to new reporting approaches).

Connections

Interdisciplinary Connections

Learning experiences illustrate strong connections within and across the disciplines. For example, students engage in

• Direct experience with real-world questions, problems, issues, and solutions that are complex and that cross discipline boundaries (e.g., students design and build a nature trail using math skills, mapping, and principles of design) as opposed to contrived or superficial themes.

• Application of skills across disciplines (e.g., questioning, estimation, and technical writing used in both social and physical sciences).

• Investigation of problems that lend themselves to the scope of interdisciplinary work (e.g., study of rural economic development from social, economic, and environmental perspectives).

• Opportunities to make connections among skills, content, and concepts within a discipline (e.g., vocabulary study connected with the history of the English language).

Relevance

Learning experiences have personal, community, or global relevance, such as

• Thematic studies that allow students to draw connections between their lives and the world beyond the classroom (e.g., the study of immigration patterns in a local town, using the "outdoor classroom" to learn the natural heritage of a local community).

• Study units that students help develop and allow them to pursue their own questions to extend or focus a unit.

• Service-learning experiences that are linked to classroom learning (e.g., writing a resource book for younger students).

• Multiple perspectives on a topic (e.g., analysis of the spotted owl issue from the perspectives of the environmentalist and the logger).

Family and Community Collaboration

The best educational climate is collaborative; school staff, families, health and human services personnel, and community members work together to support all learners. Examples of collaboration include

• Ongoing, two-way communication with parents and community members; involves sharing information, solving problems, and developing and discussing standards and criteria.

• Access to family and community resources, as well as to social agencies (e.g., counseling provided during the school day), that support high performance by all learners.

• A variety of learning environments in the community are used (e.g., libraries, lumber yards, shops, historical societies, forests, watersheds, hydroelectric dams).

• Service-learning experiences that are used to help students discover how communities work and their own role in them.

• Connections across generations (e.g., mentoring, foster-grandparenting, taking oral histories).

• Flexible scheduling for parent-teacher conferences; home visits (as appropriate) used to meet the needs of families.

• Evidence of recognition and support of diverse languages and cultures (e.g., interpreters at parent-teacher conferences and open houses).

Best Practices in the Fields of Knowledge

Arts, Language, and Literature

In addition to the best practices presented earlier, the following best practices are specific to the arts, language, and literature.

- Emphasis on multiple artistic forms and techniques.
- Emphasis on multiple reading strategies and comprehension.
- Minilessons and individual student conferences based on students' diverse literacy needs.
- Writing used as a tool for learning across the curriculum (e.g., learning logs, free writes, letters).
- Opportunities to pursue literacy through personal interests (e.g., by self-selecting topics, materials, grouping patterns, books).
- Respect and support for languages and dialects used in students' homes.
- Examples set by teachers as they model reading, writing, and discussing their thoughts with others.

History and Social Sciences

In addition to those presented earlier, best practices specific to history and the social sciences include

- Opportunities to participate in democratic processes in the school and community.
- Partnerships and internships within the community.
- Opportunities to collaborate with people of various cultures and social classes.
- Access to national and international organizations with social science resources.
- Opportunities to report on research in various forms.

Science, Mathematics, and Technology

In addition to those presented earlier, best practices specific to science, mathematics, and technology include

• Use of manipulatives and scientific tools (e.g., calculators, microscopes, graphing calculators, computer simulations, tangrams) to engage students in active, in-depth learning (e.g., investigations, problem solving).

• Frequent interactions with the natural world.

• Inquiry, investigation, and experimentation as a regular part of the science program.

• Frequent opportunities to use appropriate tools including the senses for observation and subsequent collection of data, including data that may not have been anticipated.

• Frequent oral and written interactions between teachers and students and among students to develop and extend mathematical and scientific thinking (e.g., discussions, presentations, learning logs, open-ended follow-up questions).

• Flexible grouping for investigations, problem-solving tasks, research, and experimentation.

• Teachers who display scientists' habits of mind (such as skepticism, rigor in data collection, and peer review).

• Open-ended tasks that allow students to explore and analyze scientific, mathematical, and technological questions.

• Assessment approaches that are embedded in instruction, and that require appropriate manipulatives and scientific and technological tools.

• Basic skills (e.g., measuring, recording, and computing) that are integrated with analysis, synthesis, and evaluation.

• Opportunities for students to present the results of their investigations to peers for review and critique.

Implications for the Classroom

Ultimately, the curriculum and assessment plan and the instructional guidelines are brought together in the classroom through a decision-making process involving the skillful combination and implementation of four classroom components: new units of study, existing or revised units of study, published materials, and learning experiences or routines. These components are shown in Figure 3.1.

FIGURE 3.1

Components of the Classroom Curriculum

The teacher combines these components to implement standards in the classroom:

- new units
- existing units
- published materials
- learning experiences and routines

Source: Vermont Department of Education, 1999

The teacher considers the standards he is responsible for teaching (according to the curriculum and assessment plan and the district's learning opportunities) and asks

- What published programs and materials are available through which I might teach and assess these standards?
- What existing units have I designed before that I could use again to teach and assess some of these standards?
- For which standards do I need to create new units of study?
- What learning experiences and routines do I need to redesign in a standards-based way?

Designing a standards-based classroom involves implementing the learning opportunities by making intentional links among identified standards; the strengths and needs of learners; learning-teaching activities; and assessments (see Figure 3.2). Designing standards-based learning opportunities involves recursive decision making through which standards and learning opportunities are brought to life.

Adapting Existing Units and Published Materials

A great deal of development time can be saved when existing units or published materials can be used as the basis for standards-

FIGURE 3.2

A Congruence Model

Standards-based learning requires the teacher to make continuous decisions and to offer learning opportunities that intentionally link identified standards, the strengths and needs of learners, learning and teaching activities, and assessments.

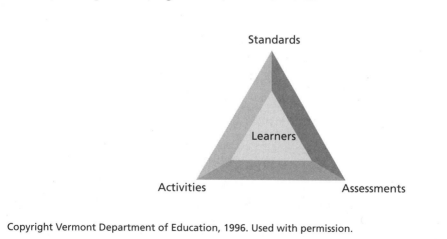

Copyright Vermont Department of Education, 1996. Used with permission.

based curriculum and assessment connections in the classroom. High-quality published materials are developed and tested far beyond what any one teacher, school, or district could ever hope to do. Units that you or other teachers have created provide activities and assessments that may be modified to provide the ongoing assessment feedback to students that is relative to identified standards. In a standards-based environment, in addition ensuring the high-quality of any materials or existing units, it is critical to examine the links between the learning and teaching activities to be used, the assessments that result, the standards that are the focus, and the interests, needs, and prior knowledge of the learners involved. It is how a unit or set of materials is implemented in the classroom that ultimately determines whether it is standards-based. The following questions can be helpful in adapting published materials and existing units of study for use in the standards-based classroom:

Standards

• What standards relate directly to the materials and assessments included in the unit or published materials?

• What other standards could be the focus of this topic or theme?

Learning and Teaching Activities and Materials

• Do the activities build in a logical progression to the identified standards?

• Are the activities sufficient to support the learning of the desired content, concepts, processes, and skills needed to attain the standards?

• Are additional activities needed to supplement existing activities?

• Are there any activities that should be removed?

• Are the activities and materials likely to be of interest to the learners involved?

• Does the activity sufficiently build student understanding of key content and concepts, or are students left with a completed activity but little or no understanding?

• Do the activities result in products and performances that can be used to assess student learning in relation to standards?

• Are the activities and materials age-appropriate for the learners involved?

• Are the activities and materials consistent with the principles in district's instructional guidelines?

• Is the written material at a reading level appropriate for the learners involved?

Assessment

• Do the assessments provide feedback in relation to the identified standards?

• Are the assessments sufficient to gather information about or document the standards that are the focus of the unit or materials?

• Are the assessments of high quality?

Learners

• Are there opportunities to find out what progress learners have already made toward attaining the identified standards?

• For learners with special needs, are activities, materials, or assessments modified appropriately?

• Are there opportunities built in for learners to be made aware of the standards that are the focus of the activities or materials and assessments?

• Are there opportunities for learners to be made aware of how they will be assessed in relation to the identified standards?

Creating New Units of Study

At times, teachers want or need to use standards to design new units of study, either because high-quality published materials are not available, they have never taught a unit to address particular standards, or a question or issue of particular interest to the students in the class lends itself to further inquiry. The questions above should also be applied when developing these units of study.

Units of study and published materials are not the only instructional processes used to teach and assess standards. Many learning experiences or routines (e.g., reading strategies, support for the writing process, scientific inquiry, or sharing time in kindergarten) cut across or are separate from units of study or published programs. As these learning experiences or routines are carried out, they are taught and assessed in relation to identified standards. The relationships must be clear and direct among identified standards; the learning and teaching activities used; the assessments provided; and the interest, needs, and level of readiness of the learners involved. Again, the questions provided earlier in this chapter can guide the planning of experiences or routines.

If the standards answer what students should learn and the instructional guidelines and classroom curriculum answer how students are to learn, then the comprehensive assessment plan and student assessment profile answer the question of how we know that students are learning.

4

The Comprehensive Assessment System

Although the media and the public often think of assessment in terms of fixed numbers representing student achievement, numbers alone do little to enhance school improvement. As an instructional leader, you must collaborate in developing a comprehensive assessment system that represents the progress in your school or district. Such a system incorporates student performance data, but the system places these data in context so that sound, data-driven decisions are used to move the school and district forward. This chapter addresses the process of developing such a comprehensive assessment system.

Leadership for Standards-Based Assessment

Figure 4.1 provides a guide for planning the components of a district's comprehensive assessment plan. Although many people think of assessment primarily in terms of the last column in this figure, student results, three other key questions should be the basis of leadership decisions in a standards-based system: (1) What are the student results? (2) Why are the results what they are? (3) How can we set priorities to improve the results?

FIGURE 4.1

Planning Guide for Comprehensive Assessment

This matrix lists examples of questions in three categories (Resources and Conditions, Programs and Practices, and Student Results) at three levels. The matrix was used to develop the Comprehensive Assessment System.

	Resources and Conditions	Programs and Practices	Student Results
	• What are the resources provided? • Does the allocation of time, people and resources align with the framework? • Do the resources support a standards-based education system?	• What are we actually doing in classrooms, at the school or district, and at the state level? • Do teaching, learning, and policy align with the Framework of Standards and Learning Opportunities? • What is the taught curriculum?	• What do students know? • What are they able to do? • Are more learners attaining the standards?
Classroom	• Demographic data • Units designed • Materials used—quantity, quality, accessibility, and equity of materials • Teacher knowledge and expertise • Vertical and horizontal alignment • Equity issues • Nature of communication with parents and community	• Completion of in-class work • Participation in out-of-class assignments and projects • Observation • Artifact analysis • Access to qualified teachers and materials • Frequency of classroom assessment of curriculum, instruction, assessment • Effectiveness of parent communication	• Student work • Classroom assessment, observations, rubrics, checklists • Departmental exams
School/ District	• Courses selected and taken • Budget information • Teacher preparation and licensing • Parent conference attendance • Parent participation in school functions • Materials purchased • Local articulated curriculum • Student-to-staff ratios	• Statewide student surveys • Middle grades self-study • Absentee rates • Discipline referrals • Suspensions from class • Expulsions • Violence incidents	• Standardized tests • Dropout rates • Student grades • District assessments • Advanced Placement (AP) scores • Honors class enrollment

Figure 4.1—continued

Planning Guide for Comprehensive Assessment

	Resources and Conditions	Programs and Practices	Student Results
School/ District	• Policies and procedures • Advanced Placement (AP) offerings • Demographic data: free or reduced lunch • Community employment figures • Nature and frequency of volunteer services • Community and business support • Nature and frequency of professional development—relationship to long-range plans, • Organization of the school day, schedules accommodate teacher collaboration • Certification of staff, years of service at school, variety of positions • Safe facilities	• Climate survey • Implementation of policies and procedures • Mobility rate • Survey of quality of professional development	• Scholastic awards • Retention rates • Comparative data among subgroups to school, district, state, national, and international results • Admission to and performance in postsecondary education • Completion of postsecondary education • Performance in workforce • Level of implementation of professional development
State	• School Quality Standards Framework Legislation • Professional Development Grants • Applicability and quality of conference, networks, grants	• School Quality Standards Survey • Learning Opportunity Surveys	• New Standards • Reference Exams: English Language Arts, Math • Math Portfolios/Rubric • Language Arts Portfolio

Source: The Center for Curriculum Renewal, 1996

In a standards-linking system, these three questions are the foundation of instructional leadership. Your job as instructional leader is to focus the system on these issues, to insist on results-driven decision-making, and to focus effort and resources on improvement.

Levels of Data Sources

Assessment decisions are made at three levels: state, district or school, and classroom. Notice that these levels refer to the level of *decision*, not necessarily the level at which an assessment is developed. For example, the decision to use a nationally developed assessment may be made at the state, district, school, or classroom level. But the results will be used differently at each level. The state may use the results to identify schools for intensive assistance. The district may use the results to compare piloting of different curricula in various schools. The school may use the results as a data source for action planning. The teacher may refer to the results in making instructional decisions. Following are additional examples of assessment decisions made at various levels.

State Level

The state may develop or adopt statewide assessments. Generally, the purpose of statewide assessments is to provide program-level information about schools, districts, and the state. This information may be used for policy and regulatory decisions at the state level, but the data also can provide important local information. Participation in statewide assessments is usually mandatory.

Local Level

To focus on particular areas—or to develop a richer, broader assessment picture beyond that offered by statewide assessments—a district or school may supplement required statewide assessment with additional assessments. Often, a district will adopt a nationally developed assessment, such as a norm-referenced achievement test or developmental reading assessment. (In the United States, schools do not have a federal mandate for specific assessments. However, some federal programs, such as Chapter 1, require a certain type of assessment.) Districts may also develop their own assessments to supplement state and national assessments. Schools and districts may decide to include assessments developed at the classroom level for broader use. Finally, assessment decisions may be made at the school or district levels as required by law or local policy. Special education assessment is an example of this type of local decision.

Classroom Level

Teachers make daily decisions related to classroom assessments. Although classroom data are primarily used to inform instruction and to communicate progress with students, parents, and other teachers, the data are also often included in school and district assessment plans.

Leadership Strategies

Classroom, local, and state data drive leadership decisions in these important areas:

- Resources: Where should dollars, time, and people be invested to maximize impact on student results?
- Programs and Practices: How can we optimize curriculum and instruction to maximize impact on student results?
- Results: What results should be our main priorities at this

time? What is our focus?

In a standards-linked system, all of these decisions are framed by standards. Therefore, standards provide the context for gathering, analyzing, and using data for program improvement decisions.

Student assessment is the foundation for decisions related to resources, programs, and practices, therefore a clear strategy for building a standards-based student assessment program is essential. The strategy includes these major components.

- Setting clear purposes for student assessment.
- Ensuring that student assessment is worth the time and effort it requires.
- Establishing the role of standards in the student assessment program.
- Developing a process for setting criteria related to standards.
- Setting performance levels.
- Developing a student assessment plan.

Setting Clear Purposes for Student Assessment

Why do we assess student performance? We assess student performance to improve education, determine success, and communicate results.

Assessment to Improve Education

At the classroom level, strong assessment improves instruction in several ways. Diagnostic assessment helps the teacher and the students determine what the students know and are able to do. Formative assessment provides information throughout the teaching and learning process and guides instructional decisions, time allocation, and selection of learning tools and resources. Summative assessment provides a measure of progress at a point in time, providing information on accountability for students and teachers. Assessment results help parents monitor their children's progress. Results also provide help and encouragement for students and families and help families make a positive connection with the classroom teacher.

At the school and district levels, assessment information provides a basis for program evaluation and program change. Student performance data drives decisions related to curriculum revision and implementation, scheduling, grouping, staffing, and resource allocation.

At the state and national levels, student performance data provides information crucial to improving education through policy and legislation.

Assessment to Determine Success.

Assessment provides a means for measuring success at several levels:

- Individual Success: How well has this student learned?
- Instructional Success: How successful was this instruction?
- Curriculum Success: How successfully is the curriculum addressing our students' learning needs?
- Program Success: How well is our instructional program working?
- Comparative Success: How well are we doing when we compare our results with the district, state, national, and international levels?

In measuring success, you must consider indicators beyond academic performance. For example, success may also be defined in terms of attendance, dropout rates, promotion and retention rates, postsecondary education, and employment. A broad definition of success helps ensure commitment to the success of all students and can highlight situations in which apparently high academic student performance is the result of large numbers of students opting out of the system.

Assessment to Communicate Results

Assessment provides a means to share results. Sharing happens in several ways. Teachers communicate assessment results to students within the classroom, providing feedback to help students direct their own learning. Educators share results with parents through report cards, progress reports, and conferences. Many schools and districts report results to the community through school report nights, media releases, and Web sites. States often communicate through school report cards and similar profiles.

These three purposes for sharing results, or similar ones, should be incorporated into the district's policy on student assessment. The purposes should also be included in documents such as faculty handbooks, student and parent handbooks, and action planning guides. The following is a sample statement of purpose.

> Communication of results is critical because communication can lead to action. The Equal Educational Opportunity Act passed in Vermont in 1997 requires that every school develop an action plan based on student performance results. This plan must be developed jointly by school and community personnel and must explicitly link curriculum, professional development, and related decisions to student results.

David Marsters, a school board member in Lincoln, Vermont, sums up the impact:

> Action planning forces us to set priorities and make decisions based on what we know about our students' performance. It has focused us as a community on data-driven improvement

for the first time in my memory. I know it will make a difference for our kids.

Ensuring Student Performance is Worth the Time and Effort

Once the purposes of assessment are established, you must
ensure that every assessment procedure serves one or more of the
purposes as efficiently and effectively as possible. The right data
guide the teacher's instructional decisions, direct the student's
learning and provide parents a window into the classroom and guide
their support of learning. For the teacher leader and administrator,
data drive local curriculum, budget, and logistical decisions. In addition, the right data drive educational policy for the state or nation.

Rarely does a single assessment tool provide equally useful data
for all purposes. Therefore, a comprehensive assessment plan com-
bining different levels of assessment for different purposes is
needed. An informal reading inventory provides key instructional
information, but does little to inform state policy. A norm-
referenced test may have little relevance to the classroom, especially if students have moved on before the results arrive.

Figure 4.2 depicts one district's estimate of how various assessments affect decision making. The first bar for each assessment
shows the district's estimate of how much the assessment is likely to
affect decisions related to individual students, the second bar represents how much the district estimates how much the assessment
will affect program decisions.

As the results portion of the comprehensive assessment system
develops, tie each assessment to one or more purposes. The overall
results section should then be evaluated to ensure that each purpose is served by the overall plan and to make certain that there are
no redundant or purposeless assessments.

FIGURE 4.2

Estimate of Relevant Information

This figure represents one district's estimate of how different types of assessment influence individual and program decisions.

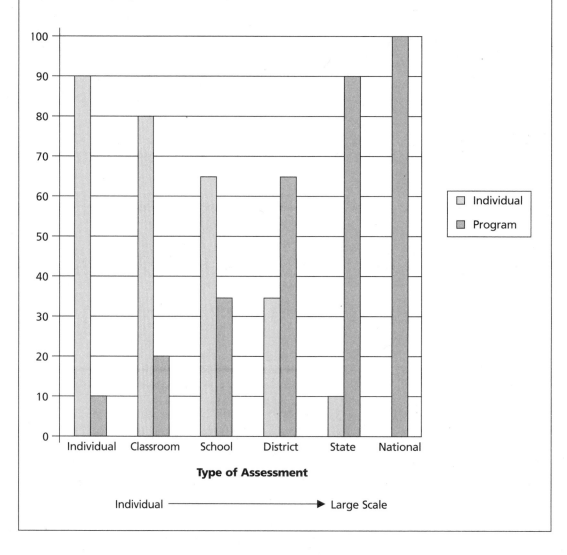

Establishing the Role of Standards

As a school leader, you must remember that each group will see the value of an assessment based on its own decision needs. Your role is to help all groups see the big picture and the multiple values of assessment data. Standards can provide a common ground for this discussion.

First, standards can be the basis for consensus as to what needs to be assessed. Many national organizations (e.g., National Council of Teachers of Mathematics and the National Association for Sports and Physical Education) have developed content standards. Most states also have developed frameworks of standards and learning opportunities. Many of these standards are subject centered. Some, like the *Vermont Framework of Standards and Learning Opportunities*, also contain "Vital Results" that cut across the curriculum. In Vermont's case, such standards include communication, reasoning and problem solving, personal development, and civic and social responsibility.

As described in Chapter 2, these standards can become the basis for curriculum development. Likewise, they can form the common link throughout a comprehensive assessment plan. For example, classroom, district, and norm-referenced assessment of problem solving may differ in many ways, but the varying assessments can focus on the same set of standards.

As described below, standards also provide the basis for establishing assessment criteria. Just as the purposes of assessment of results should be clearly stated in policy, the relationship between standards and assessment needs to be made explicit.

Developing Assessment Criteria from Standards

Agreeing on a common set of standards is important in developing a standards-based assessment system. However, standards cannot be assessed directly. Thus, the next step is to specify evidence, or criteria, to determine how teachers will know that a student's writing, experimental design, or dance performance meets a standard.

Criteria specify the dimensions or characteristics by which student work will be judged. Clear, specific criteria are important because they establish the parameters for standards-based assessment. If a standard is well written, criteria can often be found embodied in the standard. Figure 4.3 contains two examples of well-written standards encompassing criteria.

FIGURE 4.3

Two Sample Standards

Criteria for assessment may be identified by key words and phrases embedded in standards.

Standard	Criteria
Students select **appropriate technologies** and **applications** to solve problems and to communicate with an audience through **graphics, text, data, sound,** and **movement.**	Selecting technologies Applying technologies Using graphics, text, data, sound, and movement
Students plan and organize an activity by • Developing a **proposal** and obtaining approval for an activity • **Planning** and **organizing** all aspects of an event. • **Overseeing** the event through completion.	Proposal Planning Organizing Overseeing
© Harris & Carr, 1996.	

Once criteria are established, the next step is to set performance levels. How good is good enough? What level of performance defines meeting the standard? Figure 4.4 contains examples of ways in which performance levels may be specified.

FIGURE 4.4

Specifying Performance Levels

This figure illustrates four different methods of specifying performance levels for assessment, including a criterion and performance level for each.

Method	Example	
	Criterion	**Performance Level**
Present or Absent	Each paragraph has a topic sentence	Present
Percentage	Identification of variables in an experiment	80 percent of variables
Number	Supporting details in a debate	At least three per argument
Description	Asking questions about objects, organisms, and events in the environment	Ask questions combining scientific knowledge with observations

The Center for Curriculum Renewal

Sometimes performance levels are set by the state (e.g., 80 percent of students reading at grade level). Sometimes performance levels are embedded in the standards themselves. More often, though, performance levels are set locally. How good is good enough in our school and in our community?

Setting performance levels provides an excellent professional development opportunity. Educators are forced to examine each criterion directly as well as to consider the standard in terms of all criteria collectively. Examination provides a springboard for designing or selecting assessment tools because the tools must be capable of yielding information about student performance in the way specified.

Performance levels may change over time. For example, once 80 percent of students are reading on grade level, a district or school might raise the performance level to 90 percent. Or, you may decide to add an additional performance level: 80 percent will read on grade level, and 10 percent will read at least 2 years above grade level.

One middle school decided to set performance levels related to mathematics problem solving for Grade 8. In this case, the staff decided to use performance levels associated with two existing assessments. One of these is the New Standards Reference Exam, which has a problem-solving component. The middle school staff set a performance target of Level 4, as defined by this assessment, and set a target for themselves of 80 percent of their students reaching this level. They set two additional performance targets for themselves for the next three years. The first was to double the number of students performing at Level 5 (exceeding the standard). The second was to halve the number of students performing at Level 2 or lower.

The second set of performance standards relates to the Vermont Mathematics Portfolio's problem-solving section. In this case, the staff set a target for students reaching Level 3 or higher. They again set targets for increasing the number of students exceeding standards and reducing the number at the lowest level.

The process of setting performance targets led the teachers to a better understanding of the standards related to problem solving. It also forced them to review these two existing assessments carefully to make certain that they provided clear performance information related to the standards. This process led them to determine the need for a third assessment related to students' abilities to solve on-demand tasks. They were able to specify exactly what criteria these tasks needed to measure and to set performance levels related to these before developing the tasks. They then moved to the complex process of task development and benchmarking with a much clearer idea of what the tasks needed to measure than they would have had otherwise.

Developing the Student Assessment Plan

After selecting standards, defining criteria, and agreeing to performance levels, it's time to develop the student assessment plan.

Figure 4.5 is an example of a student assessment plan, adapted from the Addison Central School District in Middlebury, Vermont. In this example, note that for classroom assessments the type of assessment, rather than the specific assessment used, is included for each grade level. These types of assessment are specified by teachers in the standards-linking database described in Chapter 2. The database can be used to determine which standards are assessed using each type of assessment. Teachers may choose to detail the specific assessments used for their own purposes, but this is not necessary for the district comprehensive assessment plan.

In addition to student performance data, include other indicators of student results, such as attendance and dropout rates. In an environment where high-stakes decisions about state funding and school awards are made solely on student performance data, an unintended and undesirable outcome could be that students who perform less well are subtly encouraged to leave school and thus not negatively affect the school's overall results. Collecting data on indicators other than student performance helps to avoid this scenario.

FIGURE 4.5

Assessments of Student Academic Performance

This is an example of a comprehensive assessment plan at the district level. For each grade, it describes the assessments used at each level.

Grade	State-Mandated Assessments	Locally Chosen/Developed Assessments	Classroom Assessments
K		Early Literacy Assessment (locally developed)	Short Answer Products Performances Other
1		Early Literacy Assessment (locally developed)	Short Answer Products Performances Other
2	Early Literacy Profile	Early Literacy Assessment (locally developed) Math Assessment (locally developed)	Short Answer Products Performances Other
3		Wide Range Achievement Test Terra Nova NRT	Short Answer Products Performances Other
4	Math Portfolio New Standards Reference Exam—Math and Language Arts	Wide Range Achievement Test Math Assessment (locally developed)	Selected Response Short Answer Products Performances Other
5	Writing Portfolio	Wide Range Achievement Test Geography Assessment (locally developed) Terra Nova NRT	Selected Response Short Answer Products Performances Other
6	Science Assessment Social Studies Assessment	Wide Range Achievement Test Math Assessment (locally developed)	Selected Response Short Answer Products Performances Other

FIGURE 4.5—continued

Assessments of Student Academic Performance

Grade	State-Mandated Assessments	Locally Chosen/Developed Assessments	Classroom Assessments
7		Wide Range Achievement Test Terra Nova NRT Performance Assessments— Science and Social Studies	Selected Response Short Answer Products Performances Other
8	Math Portfolio Writing Portfolio New Standards Reference Exam—Math and Language Arts	Wide Range Achievement Test Performance Assessments— Science and Social Studies	Selected Response Short Answer Products Performances Other
9	Science Assessment Social Studies Assessment	Terra Nova NRT Performance Assessments— Science and Social Studies	Selected Response Short Answer Products Performances Other
10	Math Portfolio New Standards Reference Exam—Math and Language Arts	Performance Assessments— Science and Social Studies	Selected Response Short Answer Products Performances Other
11		Performance Assessments— Science and Social Studies	Selected Response Short Answer Products Performances Other
12		Performance Assessments— Science and Social Studies	Selected Response Short Answer Products Performances Other
All		Parent Surveys Student Surveys Teacher Surveys	Conferences

Source: Courtesy of James D. Lombardo, Superintendent of Schools, Addison Central Supervisory Union

Assessing Programs and Practices

Student results form the foundation of the standards-linking process. However, these results can only be addressed effectively in the context of learning opportunities.

Learning opportunities are the programs, practices, and resources that support student attainment of standards. As shown in Figure 4.1, (pp. 60–61), programs and practices are assessed together; resources are treated separately.

Students are sometimes held accountable for standards that are not part of the programs and practices they experience. This is an issue regarding the *opportunity to learn*, and is not an acceptable practice. When students acquire deep understanding and expertise related to standards that are not assessed, this is referred to as *opportunity to perform*. Each of these circumstances may be detected and addressed through careful program and practices assessment. Students need to have the opportunity to learn the standards and they need to have the opportunity to perform in relation to them.

The *Vermont Framework of Standards and Learning Opportunities* identifies five major categories of learning opportunities. Figure 4.6 lists these categories and related topics. The *Vermont Framework of Standards and Learning Opportunities* may be found in its entirety on the Vermont Department of Education's Web site: www.state.vt.us/educ/.

Assessing Learning Opportunities

Learning opportunities are often assessed through self-reporting by teachers and students. Although there are inherent validity questions with self-reported data, these data can be very valuable in identifying gaps and unnecessary repetitions.

FIGURE 4.6

Categories of Learning Opportunities

Here are the five categories of learning opportunities included in *The Vermont Framework of Standards and Learning Opportunities* and the specific topics for each category. The learning opportunities are essential for students to attain the standards.

Category	Topics
Access	Content
	Instructors
	Resources
	Time
	Safe and Healthy Environment
Instruction	Acquiring Knowledge and Skills
	Variety of Instructor Roles
	Multiple Student Roles
	Application and Reflection
	Adaptive Learning Environments
Assessment and Reporting	Multiple Assessment Strategies
	Criteria
	Using Assessment to Improve Instruction and Guide Student Learning
	Student Involvement in Assessment
	Effectively Communicating Assessment Information
Connections	Interdisciplinary Connections
	Relevance
	Family and Community Collaboration
Best Practices in the Fields of Knowledge	Arts, Language, and Literature
	History and Social Sciences
	Science, Mathematics, and Technology

Source: Vermont Department of Education, 1996

Appendix A provides an example of a statewide assessment of learning opportunities. This survey was part of a much larger battery used in Vermont in 1998–1999. The example is a Middle School Math Teacher Survey. Review the survey and note the type of information obtained from teachers. Do you note any trends? How might this assessment information be useful to you in reviewing the math program and its practices?

Information about learning opportunities can also be obtained locally. For example, the standards-linking database provides important information, especially related to content and assessment practice. Another valuable local source of learning opportunity data is documentation related to accreditation by regional associations of schools and colleges. Some states also include this type of data in their own school approval processes.

Learning opportunity data can also be collected at the classroom level. For example, a teacher may track the time devoted to different parts of the curriculum over a three-week period, then analyze this data in relation to the standards for which she is responsible. Or, she may ask her students to report on how their learning in a given unit of study relates to their work with their families and community. Classroom data can be valuable for the teacher in assessing her own curriculum and instructional practice and it may be aggregated across classrooms to create school or district profiles. Classroom artifacts such as assignments, assessments, and products of student learning can be collected and analyzed.

Formal observation processes have been developed for assessing learning opportunities. The Center for Science and Mathematics Program Improvement (SAMPI) at Western Michigan University has developed a set of such protocols for assessing learning opportunities in science classrooms. *Complex Instruction*, a program developed at Stanford University, also has a detailed set of classroom observation materials. These and similar processes are specifically designed to address learning opportunities, not for teacher evaluation.

Assessing Resources

Ultimately, most educational resources are connected to money, and assessment of resources related to standards is a key component of program budgets. However, in the standards-linking process, money expended is not assessed directly. Rather, resources are defined in three broad areas: materials, personnel, and time. Each of these areas was also addressed in the access section of the learning opportunities assessment and in the sample survey included in Appendix A.

Materials

Instructional materials vary widely by subject area and according to the age of students. However, they include such things as published and nonpublished print and electronic materials, technology, software, manipulatives, and kits.

You can draw on several ways to assess resources in relation to standards. One is self-reporting, as evidenced in the survey in Appendix A. A second is to complete a physical inventory of materials. A third is observation of what students actually do with the materials. This kind of observation may be achieved during supervision, evaluation, or mentoring.

Personnel

Assessment of personnel includes both documentation of numbers of personnel (often reported in terms of full-time equivalents) and data related to experience, certification, and preparation.

Statistical personnel data is frequently collected at the state and district levels.

In addition to this statistical data, schools can collect important data related to what staff members are actually doing to promote student attainment of the standards. The data may be collected by surveying teachers, paraprofessionals, and students, as well as through supervising, evaluating, and mentoring. Use this type of data to make sound decisions related to professional development (see Chapter 7) and to consider changes in staffing patterns.

Time

Time is receiving attention as a variable related to student performance. Time considerations include such issues as length of the school day and school year (for both students and teachers), scheduling, development of learning opportunities outside the school day, and year-round school options. The Connecticut Academy for Education in Mathematics, Science, and Technology (1998) has developed an excellent survey of superintendents and principals related to time issues.

What is being done with the time available? Analysis of how students and educators use of time is best accomplished at the school or classroom level. Teachers can maintain a log of their time for a specified period (e.g., three weeks), then analyze this data alone or with colleagues. Time investment can also be included as a variable in the supervising, evaluating, and mentoring process (see also Chapter 7).

The district comprehensive assessment plan is essential to improving student performance through standards linking. The plan specifies state, local, and classroom levels of data related to three key areas: resources, programs and practices, and results. However, it is a mistake to assess student results out of context. When the only data available are student results, the danger is that the wrong sorts of changes will be made. There is a tendency to start "becausing"— for example, math scores are low because we use the wrong textbook or the wrong manipulatives; we have the wrong students— when nothing has been done to determine how (or even if) the materials are being used, to determine whether teachers have had the recommended professional development, or to determine how much time is being devoted to mathematics instruction.

Comprehensive assessment is an ongoing inquiry, a process of raising questions, collecting data to provide some possible answers, and making reasoned decisions about necessary changes in programs, practices, and resources that will affect student performance.

A comprehensive assessment plan of the type described in this chapter will provide complete and coherent information to use as the basis of action planning. Chapter 5 moves from the plan to data analysis and action planning.

5

Action Planning

Action planning is the process of using your comprehensive assessment plan to set priorities for programs, practices, and resources. As we have said again and again, improving student performance is at the root of all these priorities. Schmoker (1996) summarizes this viewpoint well: Data can be "an invaluable tool, capable of telling us how we are doing, what is and is not working, and how to adjust effort toward improvement." (p. 31)

In the process we describe throughout this chapter, action planning is explicitly linked to standards at every step. Action planning focuses the educational community on measurable goals in terms of excellence (improving student performance) and equity (decreasing gaps among groups of students). Figure 5.1 lists the general responsibilities of an action planning team.

An action plan is a subcomponent of a strategic plan. A strategic plan may put student performance at its center, but the overall strategic plan includes other aspects of the school improvement process. An action plan focuses explicitly on student performance. Figure 5.2 illustrates the relationship between action planning and strategic planning.

Action Planning Teams

Action planning ultimately involves all members of the school community in implementation, but schools must first configure

FIGURE 5.1

Responsibilities of the Standards-Based Action Planning Team

Action planning focuses the educational community on measurable goals in terms of excellence (improving student performance) and equity (decreasing gaps among groups of students). The general responsibilities of the action planning team includes

- Focusing on student performance in relation to standards.
- Examining local, state, and national performance results in relation to standards.
- Placing student performance data in the context of other relevant information.
- Paying attention to trends, themes, and patterns in data over time and across groups.
- Forming hypotheses as to why student performance might be what it is.
- Setting priorities for improving student performance.
- Setting performance goals.
- Planning key priorities for improving student performance.
- Incorporating a continuous process for monitoring student performance and adjusting the action plan over time.

Source: Vermont Department of Education

teams to develop the action plan. Action planning often involves a series of nested teams. For example, a small school district may establish an action planning team for each school and one for the district. A comprehensive high school or technical center may form a team to set overall priorities, then assign content-area groups to develop specific student improvement plans. Similarly, a middle school might complement the school's team with grade-level or interdisciplinary team groups.

An action planning team typically has five to eight members. For example, a typical district-level team might include three teachers, three parents or community members (perhaps including a board member), a building-level administrator, and a central office administrator. Ideally, all team members share these characteristics

- Commitment to the action planning process during planning *and* implementation.

FIGURE 5.2

Strategic and Action Plans

An action plan is a subcomponent of a strategic plan. A strategic plan may put student performance at its center, but the overall strategic plan includes other aspects of the school improvement
process. An action plan focuses explicitly on student performance. Here is an explanation of the
relationship between action planning and strategic planning.

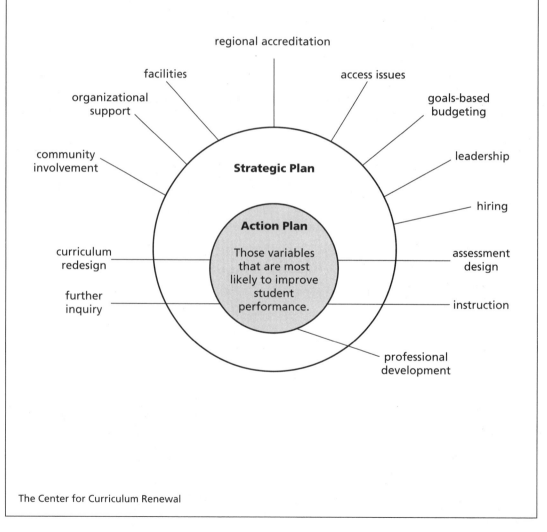

The Center for Curriculum Renewal

• Ability to communicate and make decisions within the group.

• Ability and commitment to gather information and communicate with others outside the action planning team.

• Credibility in the school and community.

The team also should include one or more members with skills and knowledge in the areas of group facilitation, data analysis and interpretation, written communication, standards-based curriculum, community expectations and priorities, and consensus building. When nested teams are part of the action planning process, each subgroup should have access to at least one member of the district's action planning team, either as a member of the subgroup or as an available resource.

In recruiting members for an action planning team, make certain that they understand the time commitment involved. A typical action planning team might have four formal meetings to develop the plan (one for each of the steps described below). If the nested team approach is used, additional meetings with subgroups is needed. The team should meet two to four times per year to monitor the plan's implementation. Ideally, all team members will participate in the annual update of the plan. Each year, some members will rotate off the teams.

Action planning requires time and effort, but this effort yields great rewards. A well-defined action plan leads to measurable improvement in student performance. The plan specifies strategies, time lines, and performance measures, therefore planners and implementers share clear expectations and knowledge of results. For these reasons, action planning teams often have high credibility in the school and the community.

A Model for Action Planning

Figure 5.3 shows a model for action planning. This model was developed by the Vermont Department of Education and the Vermont Institute for Science, Math and Technology (1999) for use in Vermont schools. The model is used in preparing action planning teams. The model also is used to introduce schools and communities to the action planning process. Though the four steps are shown in their logical order, in practice the process is iterative and steps overlap.

The following example of action planning is related to high school mathematics and was developed by Vermont Department of Education and the Vermont Institute for Science, Math and Technology (1999). This single subject example is used for clarity; in actual practice, a team would examine data across the curriculum.

Step 1

Step 1 of action planning is grounded in student performance data. This data should come directly from the student results section of the comprehensive assessment plan. Figure 5.4 (p. 90) contains an example of information related to Step 1 of the action planning process.

Three common pitfalls can occur at Step 1. One is to place too much emphasis on a single measure of student performance. In the early stages of action planning, teams often focus immediately on results of statewide assessments or norm-referenced tests. Less often, a team ignores external measures altogether and focuses only on local data. In the example above, the team examines local, state, and national data.

The second common pitfall at Step 1 is to focus on assessment results only. Student results can also be defined by measures such as

FIGURE 5.3

Action Planning Model

This action planning model can be used to introduce schools and communities to the action planning process. Though the four steps are shown in their logical order, in practice the process is
iterative and steps overlap.

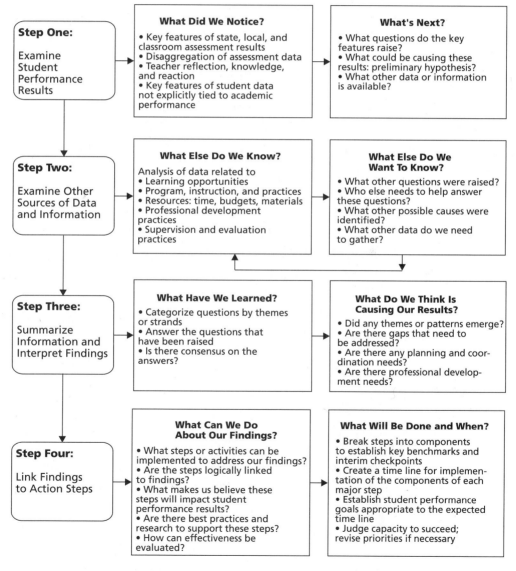

Step One:
Examine
Student
Performance
Results

What Did We Notice?
• Key features of state, local, and
classroom assessment results
• Disaggregation of assessment data
• Teacher reflection, knowledge,
and reaction
• Key features of student data
not explicitly tied to academic
performance

What's Next?
• What questions do the key
features raise?
• What could be causing these
results: preliminary hypothesis?
• What other data or information
is available?

Step Two:
Examine Other
Sources of Data
and Information

What Else Do We Know?
Analysis of data related to
• Learning opportunities
• Program, instruction, and practices
• Resources: time, budgets, materials
• Professional development
practices
• Supervision and evaluation
practices

**What Else Do We
Want To Know?**
• What other questions were raised?
• Who else needs to help answer
these questions?
• What other possible causes were
identified?
• What other data do we need
to gather?

Step Three:
Summarize
Information and
Interpret Findings

What Have We Learned?
• Categorize questions by themes
or strands
• Answer the questions that
have been raised
• Is there consensus on the
answers?

**What Do We Think Is
Causing Our Results?**
• Did any themes or patterns emerge?
• Are there gaps that need to
be addressed?
• Are there any planning and coor-
dination needs?
• Are there professional develop-
ment needs?

Step Four:
Link Findings
to Action Steps

**What Can We Do
About Our Findings?**
• What steps or activities can be
implemented to address our findings?
• Are the steps logically linked
to findings?
• What makes us believe these
steps will impact student
performance results?
• Are there best practices and
research to support these steps?
• How can effectiveness be
evaluated?

What Will Be Done and When?
• Break steps into components
to establish key benchmarks and
interim checkpoints
• Create a time line for implementation of the components of each
major step
• Establish student performance
goals appropriate to the expected
time line
• Judge capacity to succeed;
revise priorities if necessary

Source: Vermont Department of Education, 1999

attendance and dropout rates and survey data. The example in Figure 5.4 illustrates this in the section "Other Student Performance Data."

The third common pitfall in Step 1 is failing to disaggregate data. Depending on the school, you must examine data in terms of gender, ethnicity, socioeconomic background, course-taking patterns, and other measures. Failure to disaggregate data can mask key differences in student performance that should be addressed in action planning. Note that in the example in Figure 5.4, disaggregation shows significant differences in performance based on course-taking patterns.

At its first meeting, the action planning team should review the data and pinpoint key themes. Members can then develop preliminary hypotheses and questions based on the performance data. Clearly label these steps as preliminary because they will be refined or abandoned in future steps.

Once the action planning team has identified key themes in the data, these are shared with teachers and other professional staff for their reaction. This procedure is critical for three reasons: (1) teachers may make the case that the results are flawed or incomplete and point out data missed in the analysis; (2) teachers can add context to the results and may raise questions or hypotheses missed by the action planning team; (3) sharing the data with teachers lays the groundwork for continuous cooperation throughout the process and increases commitment to implementation.

Step 2

After gathering the teachers' input, the action planning team may return to the data and revise themes, questions, or hypotheses before moving to Step 2. Figure 5.5 shows Step 2 in the math scenario we are considering.

Step 2 requires the action planning team to reexamine student performance data in context. As emphasized in Chapter 4, isolating performance data can lead to false cause-and-effect assumptions, which can lead to the wrong solutions or even the wrong problem.

Step 2 requires the action planning team to examine data from the conditions and practices components of the comprehensive assessment plan. The example in Figure 5.5 shows that although a scope-and-sequence document existed at this school, it was not aligned with standards. Students in the high school had not experienced standards-based curriculum in the elementary schools, portfolio use was sporadic, and there were significant differences in course-taking patterns.

Step 3

Careful examination of learning opportunities and other conditions, practices, and resources generates another set of questions. These questions are combined with those developed in Step 1 to form the basis of analysis in Step 3. Figure 5.6 contains Step 3 of our mathematics example.

In Step 3, questions are organized into key themes. Here is the key question for the action planning team to consider: What findings have the most potential to improve student performance, both in terms of excellence and equity?

Two key themes emerged in the example in Figure 5.6. In addressing learning opportunities, the team focused on issues of equity as related to problem-solving and standards-based curriculum alignment. The team also targeted three areas for professional development, one related primarily to problem solving and two related to assessment.

Figure 5.4

Math Scenario, Step 1

The first step in action planning is to examine student performance. Note that this goes beyond analysis of test scores to include other performance data and teachers checking the data against day-to-day expenses. The Action Planning Team forms hypotheses through this analysis.

Step One: Examine Student Performance Results	→	What Did We Notice?	→	What's Next?

Student Performance	Initial Analysis and Key Features of Student Performance Results	Preliminary Hypothesis and Questions
Grade 10 NSRE Math Results Met or Exceeded: 1998 Met or Exceeded: 1999 Skills: 65% Skills: 49% Concepts: 19% Concepts: 25% Problem Solving: 16% Problem Solving: 12% Little or Below: 1998 Little or Below: 1999 Skills: 22% Skills: 41% Concepts: 63% Concepts: 52% Problem Solving: 70% Problem Solving: 75%	• Across all measures, students perform lower in concepts and application than in computation and skills • Disaggregation of results shows little difference between males and females except on the SAT, where males outperform females	• Are teachers trained in inquiry-based teaching? • Have teachers had specific instruction in use of problem-solving techniques? • Are students having the opportunity of learning experiences related to all standards?

Local Academic Assessment Results
 	
<u>Portfolio</u>
  Local scoring indicates low scores in mathematical communication
 	
<u>Norm-Referenced Assessments</u>
PSAT and SATs
  -results approximate state average for both scores and percentage of students tested
 	
CAT-5 Grades 9 and 10
  -Computation 5th stanine
  -Concepts and applications 3rd stanine
	• Disaggregation of state data shows little difference between those completing geometry in Grade 10 and those completing Algebra 1 or lower	• Do students have the opportunity to solve rich problems in all courses?

Other Student Performance Data
 	
<u>Postsecondary Survey</u>
64% of Class of 1998 attended a 2- or 4-year college
Statistics of students graduating in 1998 and attending a 2- or 4-year college:
  -28% are majoring in pure or applied science
  -2 are majoring in mathematics
  -12 are majoring in computer science or computer engineering
 	
<u>Dropout Rate</u>
  1998 rate was 7%
  No dropout had completed Algebra 2
	• Disaggregation indicates that students completing Algebra 2 or higher in Grade 10 perform significantly better than their peers.	

FIGURE 5.4—continued

Math Scenario, Step 1

Student Performance	Initial Analysis and Key Features of Student Performance Results	Preliminary Hypothesis and Questions
Teacher Reflection, Knowledge, and Reaction	• Teachers report that students tend to work for the "right answer," paying little attention to process • Teachers pay more attention to the scope and sequence of the courses they teach than to alignment with standards. They believe that each course is aligned with NCTM standards but have not examined the standards across all courses, nor have they examined classroom assessments for alignment with standards and evidence • Teachers report that many students enter grade 9 with low skills and therefore skills are strongly emphasized in courses in grade 9 and 10 • Teachers feel confident in their knowledge of content • Few teachers have experienced professional development related to problem-solving • Most teachers feel that there would be great value in reviewing student work as a means of studying problem-solving	• Is the K–12 curriculum aligned with standards? • Is there curriculum articulation, K–12?

Source: Used by permission of Vermont Department of Education and Vermont Institute for Science, Math, and Technology, 1999

Step 4

In Step 3, the number of areas to be addressed in the action plan diminishes as priorities are set. Giving up areas can be one of the most difficult processes for the action planning team. However, to be effective, the action plan must focus on a few areas, which are carefully selected as the most critical for improving student performance. These areas then become operational in Step 4. Figure 5.7 shows how this step plays out in the mathematics scenario.

Step 4 translates findings into specific activities. The action planning team must ascertain that the activities logically connect to improving student performance, that they are manageable, and that progress can be monitored during implementation. In the example in Figure 5.7, the team has developed a two-year plan focused on five areas and 10 activities. Consistent with standards linking, the action plan is systemic:

- Activities occur at all levels: classroom, school, district, and community.
- Activities are explicitly connected with standards.
- Activities are coherent. They link curriculum, professional development, and supervision and evaluation.
- Implementation is set out on a clear time line.
- Results are measurable and publicly shared.

Assessing the Action Plan

The self-assessment tool in Figure 5.8 can be used at four levels: (1) by the action planning team, before presenting the plan; (2) by the administration and school board, before approving implementation; (3) by the action planning team during implementation; and (4) by the action planning team when revising the plan.

Approving the Action Plan

Depending on the setting and the level at which the action plan is implemented, formal approval of the plan may come from the school council, faculty, principal, superintendent, or school board. The plan's quality and these factors will influence approval:

- Understanding of the action planning process.
- Consensus among the action planning team.
- Staff and administration commitment to the goals and activities.
- Clear plans for communication with the staff and community.
- A plan for monitoring and revision.

Although budget development may not coincide with this part of the process, approval of the plan also addresses at least tacit approval of resources to support it. The action planning team must make clear what people, time, materials, and dollars are needed for implementation. Often this process requires reallocation of existing resources rather than new resources; one of the key advantages of action planning is its efficiency.

Implementing the Action Plan

Implementation of action planning varies according to the specific nature of the activities and time line established in Step 4. Nonetheless, there are common elements in successful implementation.

- Involving those who will implement in determining how to implement. (Notice that the issue is not whether to implement, but how.)

FIGURE 5.5

Math Scenario, Step 2

After examining student performance data, Step 2 of Action Planning involves analysis of other sources of information. These include conditions and practices, allocation of resources, and nonacademic student data. This process generates additional questions and may inform the hypotheses developed in Step 1.

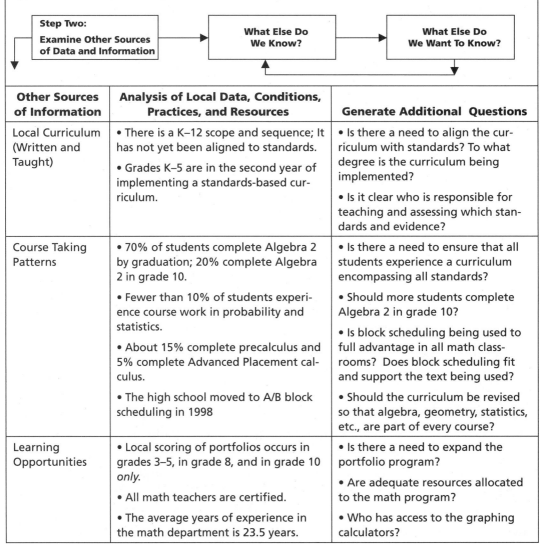

Other Sources of Information	Analysis of Local Data, Conditions, Practices, and Resources	Generate Additional Questions
Local Curriculum (Written and Taught)	• There is a K–12 scope and sequence; It has not yet been aligned to standards. • Grades K–5 are in the second year of implementing a standards-based curriculum.	• Is there a need to align the curriculum with standards? To what degree is the curriculum being implemented? • Is it clear who is responsible for teaching and assessing which standards and evidence?
Course Taking Patterns	• 70% of students complete Algebra 2 by graduation; 20% complete Algebra 2 in grade 10. • Fewer than 10% of students experience course work in probability and statistics. • About 15% complete precalculus and 5% complete Advanced Placement calculus. • The high school moved to A/B block scheduling in 1998	• Is there a need to ensure that all students experience a curriculum encompassing all standards? • Should more students complete Algebra 2 in grade 10? • Is block scheduling being used to full advantage in all math classrooms? Does block scheduling fit and support the text being used? • Should the curriculum be revised so that algebra, geometry, statistics, etc., are part of every course?
Learning Opportunities	• Local scoring of portfolios occurs in grades 3–5, in grade 8, and in grade 10 *only*. • All math teachers are certified. • The average years of experience in the math department is 23.5 years.	• Is there a need to expand the portfolio program? • Are adequate resources allocated to the math program? • Who has access to the graphing calculators?

FIGURE 5.5—continued

Math Scenario, Step 2

Other Sources of Information	Analysis of Local Data, Conditions, Practices, and Resources	Generate Additional Questions
Learning Opportunities (continued)	• Most math instruction is text-oriented. Texts are up-to-date. • Graphing calculators are available in math classrooms. • There are three computer labs in the school, with one primarily earmarked for the math and science departments.	
Survey Data	• In a follow-up study of the Class of 1998, 30% of students reported that they were well prepared in math, 32% adequately prepared, and 36% less than adequately prepared.	• Should these surveys be followed by interviews of selected students? • Should parents, college professors, and business leaders be surveyed as well?

Source: Vermont Department of Education and Vermont Institute for Science, Math, and Technology, 1999

• Committing to continuous collection of data related to both implementation and student performance.

• Committing to continuous monitoring of the plan.

• Expecting and planning for midcourse corrections and revisions.

• Maintaining focus on the plan's activities when multiple demands compete.

• Ongoing involvement of the action planning team.

• Ongoing communication with the school and community.

Problems inevitably arise when implementing an action plan. Keeping discussion focused on the goals, activities, and data helps resolve these issues. Let the data tell the story. As action planning begins to make a significant difference in school improvement, give the credit to the students and teachers making the plan work in the classroom and to those supporting the focus on student performance. Rewarding these key players builds motivation and support for the system's success.

FIGURE 5.6

Math Scenario, Step 3

The third step in Action Planning is to organize the hypotheses and questions into major themes, such as Learning Opportunities, Professional Development, and Resource Allocation.

Step Three: Summarize Information and Interpret Findings	→	What Have We Learned?	→	What Do We Think Is Causing Our Results?

Organize the Questions	Interpret Information and Data Pertinent to the Questions	Summarize Findings and Related Issues
Learning Opportunities • Do *all* students have sufficient opportunity for rich problem solving? • Does the K–12 curriculum for *all* students align with standards? • Are all teachers expected to include problem solving as part of their programs and taught curricula?	• All students do not have sufficient opportunities for rich problem solving. • The curriculum for *all* students does not align with standards. • The supervision and evaluation process does not explicitly value problem solving.	• There needs to be a concerted effort to infuse problem solving in the K–12 curriculum. • The district needs to explicitly assign standards within grade level clusters and across the high school curricula.
Professional Development • Is there a need for professional development related to problem solving? • Is there a need to analyze student work within the professional development process? • Is there a need to develop end-of-course standards-based assessments?	• There is a need for professional development related to problem-solving, K–12. • Analysis of student work should be at the center of the professional development offered. • There is a need for standards-based end-of-course assessments. Professional development should include this component.	• There needs to be an explicit professional development plan related to problem solving. • Professional development needs to emphasize analysis of student work by small groups working together. • Professional development related to developing standards-based end-of-course assessments is needed.

Used by permission from Vermont Department of Education and Vermont Institute for Science, Math, and Technology, 1999

FIGURE 5.7

Math Scenario, Step 4

The final step in action planning is to develop specific activities logically connected to student performance in the areas included in the Action Plan.

Step Four: Link Findings to Action Steps	What Can We Do About Our Findings?	What Will We Do and When?

Identify Activities Linked to Analysis of Data	Time Line for Activities	
Curriculum Revision	A. Assign standards to specific grade levels and courses, K–12.	A. Begin Summer 2000 with SDI– continue throughout the 2000–2001 year
	B. Ensure that all students, 9–12, complete a course sequence encompassing all standards. Consider whether to achieve this through integrated or traditional courses, or through a combination.	B. Begin Summer 2000 with SDI–continue throughout the 2000–2001 year
Professional Development	A. Provide embedded professional development related to analysis of student work in relation to standards. Focus this work on problem-solving and inquiry-based teaching.	A. 1999–2001 school years
	B. Participate in regional portfolio groups.	B. 1999 Ongoing
	C. Provide workshops/study groups for developing standards-based end-of-course assessments. Emphasize problem-solving in this process.	C. Begin Summer 2000. Work through 2000-2001 school year
Supervision and Evaluation	A. Use a tool for Math and Science classroom observation as part of the Supervision and Evaluation Process.	A. 1999–2000 school year
	B. Include problem-solving in goal-setting and development of professional development plans.	B. 2000–2001 school year
Community Input	A. Expand survey scope to include parents, higher education, and business leaders (as well as students).	A. Spring 2000
Monitoring Progress	A. Analyze existing and expanded classroom, local, and state data on an ongoing basis.	A. Ongoing
	B. Report progress to the community.	B. Annually, beginning Fall 2000

Source: Vermont Department of Education and Vermont Institute for Science, Math, and Technology, 1999

FIGURE 5.8

Self-Assessment Tool

This self-assessment tool may be used by the action planning team in self-assessment and by the administration and school board in approving the plan. The first column identifies the part of the Action Planning Process to be assessed. The second column identifies the criteria to be assessed. The third column provides descriptors for each criterion. The fourth column provides space for assessment. This is usually done as a yes or no evaluation, accompanied by brief comments.

Component of Action Planning Process	Criteria	Descriptor	Assessment
Assessment Needs	Data connection	Needs are identified based on data related to the standards addressed	
		Needs identified are consistent with priorities emerging from the data	
		Data includes multiple student performance indicators	
		Data includes a variety of measures, such as test results, teacher opinion, student work	
		Distribution of data is considered in establishing needs	
		Possible causes of data are considered in establishing need	

FIGURE 5.8—continued

Self-Assessment Tool

Component of Action Planning Process	Criteria	Descriptor	Assessment
	Statement of needs	Needs are described in terms of student performance	
		Needs specify areas to be addressed in the language of the standards	
Targets for Increased Student Performance	Specification of targets	Targets address improvements in student performance	
		Targets are specified in terms of percentage increase in scores OR another growth measure	
	Number of targets	The number of targets helps to focus effort, time, and resources	
Action Steps	Connection to targets	Action steps are connected to improvement in student performance as specified in the targets	
		Action steps, if implemented, likely to impact change in relation to the targets	
	Specificity	Action steps provide enough detail to focus energy, time and resources	
		Action steps specify responsibility for managing the improvement process	

FIGURE 5.8—continued

Self-Assessment Tool

Component of Action Planning Process	Criteria	Descriptor	Assessment
	Indicators	Action steps include short-term indicators of success	
Time line	Specificity	Time line includes target dates for completion of each action step and for the overall action plan	
	Flexibility	Time line permits flexibility based on short-term indicators of success	
Resources and Materials Budget	Adequacy	Human resources and materials are adequate to implement the plan	
	Focus	Human resources and materials are focused on improvement of student performance	
Overall Plan	Focus	Plan focuses on student performance Plan targets areas with highest potential impact on performance	
	Clarity	All aspects of the plan are clearly written and jargon-free	
	Evaluation	Plan includes a process for overall evaluation of implementation	
	Impact	Plan is likely to impact student achievement in relation to standards	
Source: Vermont Department of Education, 1999			

6

Reporting in Relation to Standards

Making a commitment to link standards also means making a commitment to report progress in relation to those standards. Typically, these commitments lead schools and districts to redesign their reporting systems. For example, you may have to shift your reporting so it focuses on standards. Maybe you'll have to expand the audience for the reporting to include the community at large. Or perhaps you will have to redesign the formats by which information is reported.

In general, there are two types of standards-based reporting: (1) reporting on individual student learning, and (2) reporting on the performance of the school or district as a whole. This chapter offers practical advice for reporting standards-based progress in both arenas.

Reporting on Individual Student Learning

Educators traditionally rely on parent conferences and report cards to convey information about student learning. However, these tools usually focus on compliance issues like homework and classroom behavior as much as they focus on student learning. Parent conferences are often so short that they preclude meaningful conversation about student performance. Many report cards are so spare that they include nothing more than the name of a course and the grade the student has earned. Other reports cards are over-loaded with extraneous information about field trips and books students have read.

The process of linking standards provides schools and districts the opportunity to reconstruct reporting about individual student learning so that parents, educators, and students share meaningful, useful information. The first step in this process is to expand the components of the reporting system and carefully decide what information will be conveyed and how. For example, Figure 6.1 shows a simple grid representing a district's decisions about reporting strategies. When teachers can refer to an uncomplicated resource like

FIGURE 6.1

Reporting on Student Learning

How does your school report learning? The following opportunities for reporting are available in nearly every school community. The following topics are easily addressed by using the strategies listed across the top.

	Parent Information Night	Open House	Newsletters	Rubrics	Phone Calls	Conferences	Report Cards
Information about topics, units, and materials	x	x	x				
Assessments	x	x	x			x	x
Types of instruction	x	x	x				
Performance in relation to standards				x	x	x	x
Behavior					x	x	x

Source: Washington Central Supervisory Union and the Center for Curriculum Renewal

this, they are encouraged to regularly update students and parents about curriculum, instruction, learning, and assessment.

Redesigning Standards-Based Report Cards

Report cards fit into a broader context, but they can be refined to efficiently serve their primary purpose: reporting on individual student learning. The first time we were asked to work with a school district on the design of a new standards-based report card, we found the district was using 17 different report cards in just two schools. Everyone recognized the need for a unified report card, but at the time we had no examples to offer and no clear guidelines to follow. Since then, we have worked with several districts on similar tasks, and we now have access to many samples of standards-based report cards. The following process can be adapted and used by any school or district wishing to create a standards-based report card.

Step 1: Establish a committee.

First, decide who needs to be involved in the process of revising the report card. An ideal group is made of 6–10 people, representing various grade levels, schools, and subject areas. Consider adding a parent representative to the committee or asking a separate parent group to offer insight and respond to drafts.

Step 2: Set a time line.

Reconstructing a report card typically takes three to five full-day committee meetings. After that, one to three full-day or half-day meetings are needed during the process of piloting and revising the new report card. The initial meetings can happen in one block of time, such as during a summer retreat, or they can be scheduled during the school year.

Step 3: Agree to ground rules.

Revising a report card can be an emotional process, therefore it is helpful to establish ground rules in the beginning. Figure 6.2 contains a sample set of ground rules that you might want to revise and adopt for your report card committee.

Step 4: Determine criteria for success.

This is the point to determine the indicators that will define success with the new report card. What makes a good report card? What must it contain? How will you know when the process of creating the new report card is complete? One group we worked with identified the following characteristics as being important to the

---

FIGURE 6.2

Sample Ground Rules for Report Card Committee

This sample set of ground rules may be useful in drafting, discussing, and modifying your committee's ground rules.

- Meetings will begin and end on time.
- Differences expressed in the meeting will not be carried beyond the walls of the meeting room.
- All committee members will participate fully in the work of the group, including completing outside readings and assignments agreed upon.
- To ensure the full participation of all group members in discussions and decision making, there will be no side conversations during the meeting.
- Consensus is defined as willingness to live with a decision. Every effort will be made to make decisions based on consensus of the group. When consensus cannot be reached in what the meeting facilitator deems to be a reasonable amount of time, decisions will be made by a two-thirds majority vote.
- Each member of the committee serves as a representative and will take responsibility to fully represent the views of the constituents, to share the work of the committee with them, and to seek and share their feedback.
- Committee members will rotate the responsibility for taking action minutes, recording critical decisions made by the committee.

Source: The Center for Curriculum Renewal

report card: clear and understandable, parent friendly, standards-connected, quick and manageable, consistent yet flexible, valid, and manageable format. What characteristics describe your ideal report card?

Step 5: Define the purpose of the report card.

A report card is just one part of a larger reporting system. What questions will the report card answer, and what questions will be left for other parts of the reporting system? This discussion raises broader questions about the types of information that parents in particular want to know, in particular

- What is my child doing? (topics, activities, units)
- What is my child learning? (standards, including knowledge and skills)
- How is my child demonstrating this learning? (evidence, products, performances)
- How is my child doing? (behavior, attitudes)
- Has my child improved? (progress)
- What does my child need to do to improve? (next steps)
- What can I do to help? (parental involvement)

Parents also ask one other question that we do not recommend for inclusion on the report card: "How does my child compare with other children?" A standards-based reporting system reports progress in relation to identified standards, not in relation to other children.

Step 6: Critique existing report cards.

Your existing report card came from somewhere, and presumably it contains some positive elements. What do you like about the current report card? What needs to change? Reviewing the existing report card leads to concrete conversations about desired indicators, which often leads to revising these indicators.

If you think it would be helpful to your work, review standards-based report cards from other districts. After reviewing report cards from other schools, one committee made the following observations. Although some of the observations contradict each other, the list was an important first step in clarifying what they wanted to accomplish in the design of their own new report cards. The committee determined that good report cards have the following attributes:

- Easily understandable descriptors.
- Specific to standards.
- Quick to prepare and read.
- Can be done on a computer.
- Has a personal accountability area (social-emotional issues).
- Format can be tweaked each year as a team.
- Clear language—not full of jargon.
- Standards-based without numbers (more easily understood by parents).
- Development done by the (teaching) unit.
- Does not have a space for written comments (parents come in for conferences).
- Does have space for written comments.
- Content areas are broken into subskills.
- Supplies a grid form with descriptors.
- Picture on the front of the card is appropriate.
- Flexibility to write narrative on separate sheet when it's not conference time.
- Only preparing report cards twice a year or three times a year.
- Has space for student self-assessment or student goals.
- Items match the assessments we use.
- Each broad area has a place to write a description.

OUACHITA TECHNICAL COLLEGE

Report cards that the committee decided did not answer their needs had the following problems:

- Doesn't reflect standards and state assessments.
- Contains too much technical language.
- Redundancy noted among subjects.
- Too big (11 x 17).
- List of skills is too long; some are only taught part of the year.
- Takes too much time to fill out card.
- Uses different scales (too confusing).
- Must be copied.
- Not parent friendly—a lot of information on a piece of paper (but easier to have valid data).
- Grading systems differ at each level.
- Report card filled with separate sheets of paper—from classroom teachers, art teachers, physical education staff, and more.
- Arts and physical education teachers use different approaches and scales from classroom teachers.
- Difficult to identify and convey special education classes.

Step 7: Create a mock-up.

Use chart paper, markers, scissors, and tape to create one or more mock-ups of what the new report card might look like. Sometimes committee members can work in smaller groups to complete this task, producing several variations on a similar theme. Compare, combine, and revise these mock-ups to create the first draft of the new report card. Because the samples are concrete manifestations of the principles discussed earlier in this process, critique and revision are easy. What looks good about the mock-up? What needs to change?

Step 8: Choose which standards to include.

Typically, a report card cannot include all standards that are part of the curriculum. Some information about progress with standards can be relayed directly to students in the classroom. Other information can be shared with parents through other means of reporting. The report card needs to provide a representative summary of performance across all areas of the curriculum.

Step 9: Decide what form the reporting will take.

Any or all of the following can be part of the reporting on a report card: letter grades, number grades, percentages, scales, rubrics, and narrative comments. Whatever you adopt, the language of reporting must be used consistently from school to school and from teacher to teacher using the same report card. If grading is an issue in the district, now is not the time to change the policy. Your committee is working on the report card itself, not the issue of grading. Where grades have been the only means of reporting in the past, however, a new report card focused on standards offers the opportunity to report more fully on student learning.

Although you may find it tempting to use a key that starts at 4 (exceeds the standard) and goes down to 1 (does not meet the standard), we suggest a different scale. Why? In reality, students don't meet a standard for several years. Thus, several districts we have worked with have opted to use the following language and scale:

4 = Consistently exceeds expectations related to the standard.

3 = Meets expectations related to the standard.

2 = Progressing toward meeting expectations related to the standard.

1 = Does not meet expectations related to the standard.

Step 10: Create a draft of the report card to share and revise.

Create a draft of the report card that can be shared with teachers, administrators, and parents. Format the draft to look as nearly like a finished product as possible. Sharing and critiquing the card face-to-face often works well, with each committee member presenting the card to three or four colleagues and parents. Along with the report card, share your criteria for success (see Step 4). Ask those critiquing the card to link their feedback about the card to these criteria for success. Then bring the feedback to the group as a whole and determine what changes are needed.

Step 11: Pilot the report card.

Once the committee is satisfied with the report card, try the report card in the real world. In some places we have worked, the report card is piloted only by the teachers who worked on the committee. In other schools, all teachers use the new report card all at once. Keep in mind, however, that teachers may need more time to complete the form because the report card is new. Make sure you explain the nature of the pilot clearly to everyone involved. Give parents a feedback form and clear instructions for sending back their critique.

The pilot is also the ideal time to try out new technology to simplify the whole process. Creating the report card on a computer can save time and paper and conserve teacher energy that can be channeled into the substance of the matter: reporting on student learning. However, we offer an important caution. If the report card is being completed online using a new database, spreadsheet, or other software, you'll probably run into some glitches. Planning for these glitches may help you avoid frustrations with deadlines and technical challenges.

Step 12: Review feedback, revise, and finalize the report card.

Once the pilot is complete, make the final changes to the report card. Settle decisions about substance and format.

Step 13: Identify next steps and implementation issues.

Before the committee concludes its work, invite members to reflect together on the next steps. Consider questions such as the following:

• How will all teachers have the opportunity to become familiar with the new standards-based report card?

• How will parents learn about the new report card?

• What assessments need to be in place to support the report card? Are any changes needed from past practice?

• What technology support is needed to make the use of the new report card more efficient?

• What will be the process for making revisions to the report card?

The keys to successful transition to a new report card are participation and communication. Figure 6.3 shows an example of the report card for grades 5 and 6 that the Washington Central Supervisory Union developed using this process.

Reporting on the Whole School's Performance

In Chapter 5, we discussed ways in which student performance data can be used to develop an action plan. That discussion focused on the internal use of performance data by educators and other staff members. Now we need to address the broader issue of schools and districts needing to share student performance data with the community. A clear strategy for public dissemination helps build support for standards-based learning and for the infrastructure to sustain it.

FIGURE 6.3

Sample Report Card

This sample report card is explicitly linked to standards and can be used an as exemplar as you develop a standards-based reporting system. You are encouraged to review as many report cards as you can early in the process.

Quarters	1	2	3	4
Reading/Literature Standards				
Uses a variety of reading strategies				
Comprehends grade level material				
Reads grade level material accurately				
Reads a variety of materials				
Responds to literature (oral, written, artistic)				
Writing Standards				
Uses the writing process (drafts/revises/edits)				
Writes for a variety of purposes (response to literature, reports, narratives & procedures)				
Uses correct punctuation & capitalization				
Applies spelling skills				
Writes legibly using proper size and spacing				
Listening & Speaking Standards				
Actively listens & responds				
Expresses ideas clearly				
Participates in group discussions				
Math Standards				
Adds accurately to 18				
Subtracts accurately from 18				
Computes accurately				
Applies number concepts (estimating, place value, fractions, counting)				
Applies geometric concepts (identify, classify, compare shapes)				
Applies measurement concepts (linear, time, money)				
Uses a variety of grade appropriate mathematical, language, symbols, and representation				

FIGURE 6.3—continued

Sample Report Card

Quarters	1	2	3	4
Science Standards				
Uses scientific method (asks questions, observes, records, and interpret results)				
Demonstrates knowledge of content standards				
History & Social Science Standards				
Demonstrates knowedge of history standard				
Demonstrates knowledge of geography standards				
Demonstrates knowledge of citizenship standards				
Research & Information Technology Standards				
Explores technology				
Explores library resources*				
Reasoning & Problem Solving Standards				
Uses a variety of strategies to solve problems				
Personal Development & Social Responsibility Standards				
Interacts respectfully with others				
Works effectively in groups				
Makes an effort to solve social problems				
Participates appropriately				
Follows directions				
Works independently				
Completes high-quality daily work				
Completes homework assignments				

Source: Washington Central Supervisory Union

KEY
1. Does not meet expectations
2. Progressing toward meeting expectations
3. Meets expectations
4. Consistently exceeds expectations
NA = not assessed in this quarter
* = Possible collaboration with Library Media

In the following sections we describe four stages in developing a public dissemination strategy. Stages 1 and 2 lay the groundwork for the public engagement described in Stages 3 and 4. Although the beginning of each stage usually occurs in the order listed, the process is recursive and continuous. Returning to these four stages on an ongoing basis is important because each stage provides essential support for the others.

Stage 1: Public Awareness of Standards

Many schools and districts ignore one obvious point: Members of the public have a hard time understanding standards-based assessments unless they understand the standards. Before you can do any reporting, you must build public awareness of your standards.

Be certain to focus your work on building awareness of standards. You are not inviting parents and businesspeople to review and critique each standard. Instead, focus attention on questions like these:

- What are standards?
- Where did they come from?
- What is their purpose?
- Are they challenging?
- How are they changing education?

Parents and members of the business community often have additional questions. For parents, these questions usually include the following: What changes will I see in my child's classroom? What can I do to help my child achieve the standards? What will be the consequences if my child does not achieve the standards?

Members of the business community might pose questions related to workplace readiness. For example, New Jersey adopted Cross-Content Readiness Standards (New Jersey State Board of

Education, 1996) describing five key workplace standards: self-management skills; critical thinking, decision-making, and problem-solving skills; career planning and workplace skills; safety principles; and technology and information. Similarly, Vermont (Vermont Department of Education, 1996) has adopted Vital Results Standards in four areas: communication, reasoning and problem solving, personal development, and social responsibility. Standards like these are a high priority for the business community, and business leaders and employers may have questions about them.

When you communicate standards to the public, define a key core message. In the state of Washington, for example, the School Improvement Effort (Washington Partnership for Learning, 1999) has three steps:

1. Set clear and challenging academic standards.

2. Measure how well students and schools are meeting the standards.

3. Make both schools and students accountable for improved performance.

These steps appear in virtually every communication related to standards and results. The core message never varies.

You can use a variety of ways to build public awareness of standards. Remember that the goal is not to have the public know the list of standards; instead, your goal is to answer key questions about the standards. Stories are a useful tool for achieving this goal. What are real examples of how standards are transforming learning in your school? Convey your stories and message through various print media such as press releases, mailings, bookmarks, and newsletters.

Meetings are another effective way to share standards. For example, the New Jersey Math Coalition has developed the FANS program: Families Achieving the New Standards (Rosenstein,

1998). Their goal is to reach half New Jersey's parents through 90-minute workshops. They have developed a protocol and materials for these workshops including video, print materials, and hands-on work by the parents. Many local schools and districts have developed similar programs or have revised traditional programs like Family Science to incorporate standards. Vermont educators have provided sessions related to standards awareness and analysis of results for the IBM Corporation at the workplace during the workday. Meetings like these are valuable opportunities to heighten awareness of standards and lay the groundwork for ongoing support.

Web sites are another means of providing in-depth information about standards. Many states and districts include information about standards on their home pages. Please note that, unless your standards are locally developed, it's important to provide links to the appropriate state and national Web sites rather than to post someone else's standards directly on your site. Why? As the standards evolve, the task of continuous updating belongs to those who are developing the standards, not you. Providing links to the original source of the standards ensures your site doesn't become cluttered with stale information.

Stage 2: Public Awareness of Assessment Tools and Procedures

Reporting the results of standards-based assessments is greatly enhanced when parents and other adults have some awareness of the assessments. This is particularly true for rigorous, statewide standards-based assessments that carry a different message from norm-referenced tests. A community that is complacent about above-average performances on norm-referenced tests may be shocked when few students meet the standard on a standards-based assessment.

One of the most compelling ways to engage the public in test results is to have adults take the actual test that students took. Community members are often amazed at the depth and complexity of the questions. When adults take a test themselves, they gain a better understanding of how rigorous the standards and assessments are. At least three states (Maine, North Carolina, and Washington) have teamed with fast-food restaurants to place test items on tray liners. Some communities have held game-show contests in local malls, pitting school board members against local celebrity teams using test questions. (These communities also provide written information about standards at the same time). Challenges to governors, legislators, and other policy-makers have been successfully used as promotional vehicles. Vermont posts assessment tasks on the Web along with student work to benchmark it. All these techniques can provide adults direct experience with assessments as a context for results.

Stage 3: Sharing Assessment and Related Results

Stage 3 includes two parts: setting the context for reporting and actually reporting the results.

Vermont schools are required by statute to annually report student results in relation to standards. This type of mandate is not universal, but the need for this kind of reporting exists in every state. As discussed in Chapter 5, any reporting must be done in context. The press often reduces this reporting to a ranked list of numbers; schools and districts themselves must provide the total picture.

Although the details of the total picture will vary, here are some types of data to consider for a complete school profile. (The examples in each area are neither all-inclusive nor appropriate for every profile.) You will recognize that the categories parallel the data organization in Figure 4.1 (pp. 60–61).

Resources and Conditions

- Students (Who are our students? Demographics, developmental assets, health information, percent receiving special education and support services, numbers in advanced placement courses)

- What is the make up of our community? (Demographics, parental participation in school functions, school and community partnerships)

- Who are our staff? (Numbers, academic preparation and licensing, years of service, standards and content-related professional development)

- What are our resources and how are they deployed? (Class size, staffing patterns, time allocation, schedules, courses offered and taken, support services, budget allocations, grants, and other external support)

Programs and Practices

- Instructional practice (Standards-based instruction and assessment)
- Support services
- Supervision and evaluation practices
- Professional development (What's offered and the related effects)
- School climate survey (Results)
- Student management systems and results (Attendance, referrals, suspensions, expulsions)
- Information technology (Computers, print and nonprint media)
- Administration
- Strategic plan
- Results
- Local assessments

- Grades
- Statewide assessments
- Standardized tests
- National and international assessments (e.g., National Assessment of Education Progress, Third International Math and Science Study)
- Advanced placement
- SAT scores
- Exit data (entrance and performance in workforce, college admission and completion)
- Dropouts
- Retentions

Once you complete a school or district profile, you can target key results in context. For example, you may create a press release around your reading data including test results, classroom practices, and research in the area of reading. Or you might sponsor a math night at your school where you present local data, national data, examples of math problems from the assessments, and discussion of the math standards and curriculum.

When reporting student performance data, try to anticipate public questions related to the results. The Vermont Department of Education (1999) has developed an Internet-based School Improvement Support Guide (http://data.ed.state.vt.us/apg/index.html) from which citizens can find answers to key questions about their schools' performance. At this writing, 8 of 12 questions are active, but all 12 are listed in Figure 6.4 (p. 121) for your consideration as you frame questions for your data.

Vermont's *School Improvement Support Guide* (Vermont Department of Education, 1999) provides excellent models of how to graphically display your data. Line graphs, bar graphs, pie charts, and tables each have their advantages for displaying data, and can greatly enhance your message.

- Line graphs are best used to show the relationship of two variables, such as number of math courses taken to SAT scores or enrollment over time. Line graphs are not often used in school profiles because few student performance variables display a linear relationship to single variables.

- Pie charts are used to display the size of the parts of a single variable to the whole. A pie chart may be used, for example, to display the school budget or to represent activities of graduates after high school.

- Bar graphs are the most commonly used graphic display in reporting student achievement data. They can be used effectively to show performance on the same measure over time and to show performance on a set of measures in the same year.

- Charts and tables are also commonly used in school profiles, particularly when a large amount of information needs to be presented in one graphic. An example would be a display of all standardized test data for a school or district.

As you prepare to report your data, check the way that graphics are used in answering the questions posed on Vermont's *School Improvement Guide*. We can also recommend two other excellent resources for data display. The Math League Web site has a clear, concise explanation of use of various types of graphs and includes examples: http://www.mathleague.com (2000). The Addison Central Supervisory Union includes a *Profile of Schools* (Addison Central Supervisory Union, 2000) on its Web site (http://www.acsu. k12.vt.us) and includes excellent graphic displays of student data in a real-life example of a student performance profile.

FIGURE 6.4

Questions for School Performance

These questions can be used as a springboard for examining student performance.

• What percentage of students met or exceeded the standards on state assessments this year?
• What percentage of students scored in the lowest two performance levels on state assessments this year?
• What is the distribution of scores across all performance levels?
• Are there gender differences in performance?
• How did our students do in mathematics and science content areas this year?
• How does our performance compare to that of schools in our district or supervisory union, statewide results, and other schools' results this year?
• How did we do compared with similar schools on the state assessments this year?
• Are we making progress toward all students meeting or exceeding state standards?
• Are we reducing the percentage of students in the bottom two performance levels?
• What percentage of our students participated in the state assessments this year?
• Are we making progress toward all students participating in the state assessments?
• Did our school make Adequate Yearly Progress this year?

Source: Vermont Department of Education, 2000. Available online at http://data.ed.state.vt.us/ape/index.html.

Stage 4: Developing Public Involvement in Improving Standards-Based Learning

Publicity about results often generates action. Some parents, community members, and business leaders seek ways to become involved in the schools once they see the data. Many more people offer assistance if you ask about and provide avenues for community involvement. Reporting is not only the chance to offer information; it's an opportunity to reach out to the community and invite their involvement.

As discussed in Chapter 5, the action planning process brings community members and educators to the table to analyze data and establish priorities and strategies for improving student performance. Direct involvement in decision making is powerful, though it involves relatively few people. How can you engage many more in this important mission?

Washington Partnership for Learning (1999) has developed suggestions that can help parents and businesses get involved in standards. (They also publish a list for educators.) Their lists are excellent because they contain concrete, doable steps that can make a difference. Their lists also illustrate how reporting in relation to standards gives everyone a role in supporting improved student performance.

FIGURE 6.5

What Parents Can Do to Support Higher Standards

Parents can always be involved in the education of their children. The most important ways of being involved and supporting higher standards are listed below.

- Talk to and work with your child's teacher.
- Read.
- Practice writing at home.
- Make math part of everyday life.
- Ask your child to explain his thinking.
- Use the community as a classroom.
- Help other parents understand changes to a standards-based environment.
- Look for a schoolwide commitment to the standards.
- Acknowledge a good job when you see it.

Source: Washington Partnership for Learning, 1999

7

Professional Development, Supervision, and Evaluation

In a standards-based environment, adult needs, goals, and satisfaction are no longer the center of professional development. Over time, professional development, supervision, and evaluation all evolve to focus on improvement of student learning in relation to standards. These student learning needs emerge from careful analysis of student performance data in the context of action planning, as described in Chapter 5. This chapter considers several guiding principles for standards-based professional development along with examples of best practice.

Guiding Principles

As discussed in Chapter 1, Loucks-Horsley and colleagues (1998) have identified seven key principles for effective teacher development programs. These principles were initially developed for effective professional development in math and science. Here we address those principles in the context of standards linking.

Principle 1: Effective professional development experiences are driven by a well-defined image of teaching and learning.

In a standards-linking system, the image of teaching and

learning is grounded in standards. Schools and districts make a series of decisions to define how standards will be implemented, including

- Who is responsible for what standards? (See Chapter 2)
- How will we define instructional guidelines for the attainment of standards? What will teachers and students do in the classroom? (See Chapter 3)
- How will the standards be assessed? What criteria will be used to define attainment of standards? What performance levels will be expected? (See Chapter 4)
- What do data tell us about current attainment of standards? What are implications for teaching and learning? (See Chapter 5)

Professional development decisions also must emerge directly from the careful consideration of these questions. Indeed, the decision-making processes involved are themselves a foundation of professional development in a standards-linking system.

Principle 2: Effective professional development experiences provide opportunities for teachers to build their knowledge and skills.

As described in Chapter 5, action planning targets explicit areas for improving student performance. By linking professional development priorities to the action plan—and by focusing time, energy, and resources on these areas—a school or district can provide long-term professional development related to these areas.

For example, consider the action plan in Chapter 5. Student data at this high school showed a need for improvement in the targeted area (problem solving). The school's plan details three strands of professional development over two years: analysis of student work, portfolio development, and development of end-of-course assessments. Each of these areas focuses on building teachers' abilities to instruct and assess problem solving. By providing long-term, multifaceted professional development opportunities to its high school math teachers, this school is likely to influence all teachers working with students in the area of problem solving.

Principle 3: Effective professional development experiences use or model the strategies teachers will use with their students.

The modeling we describe here begins with the emphasis on standards. Just as teachers will be expected to make daily classroom decisions based on standards, professional development decisions must be standards driven. In the example in Chapter 5, student performance is the foundation of staff development. Teachers will collaborate in analyzing student performance, reflect individually on the implications of their students' performance for their teaching, study and research content and pedagogy based on identified needs, and maintain a focus on results. All of these reflect best practices in a standards-based classroom.

Principle 4: Effective professional development experiences build a learning community.

A standards-linking system builds its learning community on these key assumptions:

• Standards focus learning for all learners (children and adults).

• All learners construct new learning.

• All learners learn from and with others and through research and reflective practice.

• Assessment and knowledge of results drive learning decisions.

Professional development, classroom practice, and all schoolwide decisions must reflect these assumptions. Then, the coherent approach provided by standards linking can build structures and support to sustain a learning community focused on student performance. (This area is discussed in detail in Chapter 1.)

Principle 5: Effective professional development experiences support teachers to serve in leadership roles.

Teachers assume formal leadership roles through mentorships, peer evaluation, and other forms of colleague consultation. Teachers should be key decision makers on action planning teams, choosing areas of focus based on student performance. Teachers also must take leadership roles in assigning standards, developing instructional and assessment strategies, and analyzing student work. Teachers can conduct research in their classrooms and share results. In sum, teacher leadership is at the core of the standards-linking system.

Principle 6: Effective professional development experiences create links to other parts of the educational system.

Standards linking is a systems approach, therefore all components and decisions affect all other areas. This concept is explored in detail in Chapter 1.

Principle 7: Effective professional development experiences are continually assessed and improved.

In a standards-linking system, effectiveness is measured in terms of gains in student improvement. As described in Chapter 5, this may include excellence gains (gains for all students), equity gains (narrowing of gaps in achievement differences among students), or both. The action planning process requires ongoing monitoring of student improvement gains and continuous system revision based on results.

Examples of Best Practice

As these seven principles illustrate, professional development in the standards-linking system recognizes the primary role that continuous adult learning plays in improving students' learning. Following are concrete examples of professional development processes that we have found work well in a standards-based environment. This list is not exhaustive. We also acknowledge that traditional options such as coursework, workshops, and inservice days do have their place in professional development planning as valuable formats described in great detail in other works. In this list, however, we have chosen to describe processes and practices that have been especially beneficial to our work with standards linking.

Focus on Student Work

Lewis (1998) describes two protocols for bringing teachers together for collaborative discussion of student work. The first, developed by Ruth Mitchell and the Education Trust, focuses on the quality of classroom assignments and their direct connection with standards. We have found this process to be valuable with teachers in grade-level and middle school teams and high school departments. These are the steps of the discussion process, which takes 90 minutes to 2 hours:

1. We all complete the assignment.
2. We identify the standards that apply to this assignment.
3. We generate a rough scoring guide from the standards and the assignment.
4. We score the student work, using the guide.
5. We ask: Will this work meet the standards? If not, what are we going to do about it?
6. What action can we plan at the classroom, school, district,

and state levels so that students meet the standard on assignments like this?

Lewis has described a protocol developed by Project Zero at Harvard. This process focuses directly on student work rather than the assignment itself. Focusing on student work in relation to standards is essential for two reasons. First, this focus shifts conversation from the standards themselves to the work that represents students' attainment of standards. Such a shift is essential to move the system to focus on what is done, not what is expected. Second, by examining student work, teachers create a forum for reflecting on their own practice through collaborative analysis of the work of others. What kinds of assignments do they give? What kinds of work do their students produce? How carefully do they consider standards in their classrooms? As they become more comfortable with collaborative analysis and more confident in their own work, teachers can begin to offer their own assignments and the work of their own students for analysis and discussion.

Data-Driven Dialogue

Laura Lipton and Bruce Wellman (1999) have developed a collaborative learning process for data-driven dialogue. Their Pathways to Understanding model organizes dialogue around three iterative steps: activating and engaging, organizing and integrating, and exploring and discovering. Lipton and Wellman also identify four strategies for supporting growth through collaboration: managing, modeling, mediating, and monitoring. Each of these strategies emphasizes the importance of incorporating reflective practice into collaboration.

Lipton and Wellman's work was instrumental in our development of the action planning model described in Chapter 5. Their work also has been used extensively in the professional development of curriculum leaders in Vermont. We cannot emphasize enough the importance of building structures and strategies for collaborative analysis of data, and Lipton and Wellman's work has proven extremely effective in this process.

End-of-Course Assessments

Mike Schmoker (1999) has developed a process for leading high school faculty through development of standards-based end-of-course assessments. Engaging high school faculty in this process has several advantages. Teachers work collaboratively on a concrete task with immediate application. The process of identifying standards for end-of-course assessment also increases focus on standards in daily teaching and assessment. A series of standards-based end-of-course assessments can be valuable in analyzing opportunities for all students to learn in relation to standards. The tests provide key local components of the student performance profile and comprehensive assessment plan.

We have used Schmoker's process successfully in high schools and in developing year-end mathematics assessments in 2nd and 6th grades. His process has provided a practical professional development process yielding great benefit in terms of focusing attention on standards and student performance.

Standards into Action

The IBM Reinventing Education project collaborated with the Vermont Department of Education and others to produce Standards into Action. This software enables teachers to develop standards-based units of study incorporating assessment tools, published materials, and existing teacher-developed materials. The software's templates, databases, and capacity for sorting and sharing information make it an invaluable professional development tool. (For more information on Standards into Action, contact the Vermont Department of Education.)

Study Groups

Murphy (1999) describes a whole-faculty study group process. Every faculty member participates in a series of small groups with no more than six members. The groups meet regularly to focus on student needs. Murphy describes 15 guidelines for these study groups, one of which is a focus on curriculum and instruction. Although the model is not explicitly designed for use in a standards-based setting, study groups can productively focus on standards. (For more information on whole faculty study groups, contact the National Staff Development Council.)

Personal Learning Plans

The National Institute for Community Involvement (NICI) supports Professional Development Schools where K–12 faculty, higher education faculty, and prospective teachers work together in school settings. NICI emphasizes development of personal learning plans (PLPs) incorporating institutional, professional, and personal goals. Each of these links to standards in terms of learning results, learning opportunities, and learning climate. These learning plans are especially powerful because PLPs are also used by K–12 students in the Professional Development Schools.

Vermont Math Initiative

The Vermont Mathematics Initiative (VMI) "provides teachers with a broad and deep understanding of mathematics to enable peer professional development in support of standards-based learning and enhanced student learning of mathematics" (Gross, 1999,

p. 1). The three-year program emphasizes the collaboration of professional mathematicians and elementary teachers. Leading with math content, the program also focuses on math pedagogy and leadership. Participating teachers can complete a master's degree or certificate of advanced study in K–6 mathematics teaching.

VMI is representative of recent initiatives that ground the study of teaching and learning in deep understanding of content. These programs are especially important as the complexity of content knowledge required by standards continues to increase, especially at the elementary level.

Teacher Associate Program

The Vermont Institute for Science, Math, and Technology (VISMT) directs an associate program for teachers, higher education faculty, administrators, and others seeking leadership roles in standards-based curriculum implementation. Curriculum implementation associates work four days per week on statewide implementation initiatives and one day a week in their schools or districts.

Other curriculum implementation associates work primarily in their local settings, but they also participate in statewide initiatives. All associates receive extensive professional development in content, use of technology, standards-based curriculum and assessment, and leadership, and they work collaboratively with statewide and local leaders. After one or two years as associates, most participants move into curriculum leadership positions in their schools or districts; others continue to work statewide.

The associates model is a very intense leadership experience for practitioners in K–12 and higher education. This model also has proven very effective in building local capacity for leading standards-based systemic change.

Planning for Professional Development

A professional development plan begins with a vision. As emphasized throughout this chapter, this vision must focus on the improvement of student learning. Educators must believe that student learning will improve as teachers and administrators receive the training and support they need to better teach and assess standards. The vision also must emphasize the priority of continuous learning for all learners in the system, both staff and students.

A professional development needs assessment serves two purposes. First, the assessment identifies needs for standards-related professional development as described by staff. Second, the assessment identifies resources for professional development. The needs assessment should be combined with priorities that emerged from action planning (see Chapter 5) to form the foundation of professional development planning.

Once priorities are established, schools or districts can develop and implement a professional development plan. The questions listed in Chapter 1 also can be used to develop a long-range professional development plan tied explicitly to improving student performance.

Supervision and Evaluation

The primary purpose of any supervision and evaluation system should be to continuously improve the instruction provided to each student. Supervision and evaluation also play a significant role in ensuring accountability. An effective system both motivates educators to strive for higher levels of knowledge and performance and provides the necessary support to make continuous professional growth attainable. In addition, an effective system responsibly provides opportunities for improvement for those whose performance does not meet stated expectations.

Any credible process of supervision and evaluation must begin by acknowledging the inherent complexity of educators' multifaceted jobs. Supervision and evaluation also must recognize and make provisions for educators' varying professional needs and aspirations at different stages in their careers. A high-quality system is collaborative, encouraging ongoing, substantive dialogue about best practices in education. The system also must use multiple sources of data and feedback.

As shown in Chapter 1, three important aspects of the supervision and evaluation cycle are now typical in many school districts: goal setting or formative evaluation, colleague consultation and support, and administrative or summative evaluation. These areas create the context in which educators can focus specifically on standards. The following questions are also helpful in achieving this goal.

Which standards focus supervision and evaluation?

The predominant focus of supervision and evaluation is on standards for student learning, whether these are local, state, or national. In addition, commitments to instructional guidelines such as those described in Chapter 3 help to focus the goal-setting process. Standards for professional practice and standards for school performance may also be used. For example, the Vermont Standards Board for Professional Educators (1999) has adopted *Standards for Vermont Educators: A Vision for Schooling*. This document presents standards and principles to guide the preparation of new teachers and administrators and the continuing development of professional educators. These standards are shown in Figures 7.1 and 7.2. Using public standards as the basis for supervision and evaluation clarifies expectations and enhances professional discourse in schools.

How are the identified standards used in determining the focus for supervision and evaluation?

Not all standards can be the target of each phase of a supervision and evaluation cycle. Therefore, it is necessary to set goals that the parties involved can use to guide their interactions in the interest of professional growth. A good goal is

- Measurable: By what means will we know if the goal is accomplished?
- Targeted: What exactly will happen?
- Connected: What specific standards will be realized?

What does the standards-based classroom look like?

Teachers and administrators from several districts are working together from the standards and instructional guidelines to build more detailed rubrics to guide classroom observations. These guides provide a range of performance in relation to the desired expectations. An excellent resource for incorporating such rubrics in a local supervision and evaluation system is Charlotte Danielson's *Enhancing Professional Practice: A Framework for Teaching* (1996). Danielson's framework divides the complex activity of teaching into 22 components clustered into 4 domains of teaching responsibility: planning preparation, classroom environment, instruction, and professional responsibilities. Danielson's follow-up book, *Teacher Evaluation to Enhance Professional Practice* (Danielson & McGreal, 2000), provides a wealth of information on how to evaluate teachers.

Our colleagues in the Windsor Southwest Supervisory Union in Chester, Vermont, used Danielson's work and other resources to

FIGURE 7.1

Five Standards for Educators

The Vermont Standards Board adopted these standards for professional educators. Use these standards to frame discussion of your standards for professional educators.

LEARNING
(Content Expertise)
Each educator continues to acquire new learning in the content area or areas of professional endorsement and reflects this new learning in professional practice. Each educator is knowledgeable about the content requirements of his endorsements.

PROFESSIONAL KNOWLEDGE
(Methodology and Pedagogy)
Each educator continues to acquire knowledge in best practices in teaching and the learning process, so as to improve learning opportunities for all students.

COLLEAGIALITY
Each educator works collaboratively with colleagues at local, state, and national levels to improve student learning through implementation of national standards, state standards, district goals, school goals, and action plans.

ADVOCACY
Each educator works to improve the educational health of learners, and promotes fairness and equity for all students and members of the educational community. The educator engages the family and the community in partnerships to promote student learning.

ACCOUNTABILITY
Each educator carries out professional responsibilities ethically. Each educator demonstrates professional growth over time in each of the Five Standards for Educators through a professional portfolio that includes evidence of rigorous professional development, reflective practice, and adapting practice to improve student learning. A portion of each educator's IPDP and professional portfolio will be connected to his school's initiatives for improving student learning.

Adapted from Vermont Standards Board for Professional Educators, 1999

create rubrics tied directly to learning opportunities (such as those shown in Chapter 3) and to Vermont's Standards and Principles for Professional Educators (shown in Figures 7.1 and 7.2). Figure 7.3

FIGURE 7.2

Principles for Educators

The Vermont Standards Board adopted the following principles for professional educators. Use these principles to lead discussion on adopting your own principles for educators.

LEARNING
Principle 1
The educator has knowledge and skills in the content area or areas of endorsement at a level which enables students to meet or exceed the standards represented in both the Fields of Knowledge and the Vital Results of *Vermont's Framework of Standards and Learning Opportunities.*

PROFESSIONAL KNOWLEDGE
Principle 2
The educator understands how individuals learn and grow and provides learning opportunities that support intellectual, physical, social, and emotional development.

Principle 3
The educator understands how individuals and groups differ and creates equitable instructional opportunities that respond to the needs of all students.

Principle 4
The educator uses a variety of instructional strategies to provide opportunities for students to meet or exceed the expectations in *Vermont's Framework of Standards and Learning Opportunities.*

Principle 5
The educator creates a classroom climate that encourages respect for self and others, positive social interaction, and personal health and safety.

Principle 6
The educator implements, adapts, revises, and, when necessary, creates curriculum based on standards, current knowledge, student needs, and interests.

Principle 7
The educator uses multiple assessment strategies to evaluate student growth and modify instruction to ensure the continuous intellectual, social, physical, and emotional development of every student.

Principle 8
The educator uses research, data, including student performance data, and other resources to improve practice.

FIGURE 7.2—continued

Principles for Vermont Educators

Principle 9
The educator integrates current technologies in instruction, assessment, and professional productivity.

COLLEAGUESHIP
Principle 10
The educator works as a team member and forms professional relationships with colleagues as part of a system and actively implements the school's goals and articulated curriculum.

ADVOCACY
Principle 11
The educator establishes collaborative relationships with school colleagues, parents, agencies, and others in the community at large to support students' learning and well-being.

Principle 12
The educator recognizes multiple influences on students inside and outside the school and accesses appropriate systems of support for students.

Principle 13
The educator understands laws related to student and educator rights and responsibilities and treats students and colleagues fairly and equitably.

ACCOUNTABILITY
Principle 14
The educator grows professionally, through a variety of approaches, to improve professional practice and student learning.

Principle 15
The educator assesses student progress in relation to standards and modifies plans and instruction to improve student learning.

Principle 16
The educator maintains useful records of student work and performance and knowledgeably, effectively, and responsibly communicates student progress in relation to standards in a manner easily understood.

Source: Adapted from Vermont Standards Board for Professional Educators, 1999 (pp. 139–143) shows part of a rubric these educators designed for instruction.

Rubrics used in supervision and evaluation should be tied directly to existing policies and standards. Rubrics should be developed and critiqued by the teachers and administrators who will use them. Together with the standards, rubrics should define what the standards-based classroom is expected to look like.

How are the standards used in the supervision and evaluation process: self-assessment, goal setting, colleague consultation, and summative evaluation?

Standards can be translated directly into questions that guide each of these supervision and evaluation processes.

Self-Assessment
- On which standards am I focusing?
- What are my strengths?
- In what areas do I need to focus improvement?
- What supports do I need to make the necessary changes?

Goal Setting
- For which standards do goals need to be set?
- Which standards present the greatest challenge?
- What tools will be used to measure accomplishment of the goals?

Colleague Consultation
- In relation to which standards may we best support each other?
- What strengths and needs do we bring to the interaction?
- What resources might we use?
- What is our experience with collaboration?

FIGURE 7.3

Rubric for Instruction

This excerpt is taken from a rubric developed by a school district to define what the standards-based classroom should look like. This type of rubric can be used for teacher self-assessment, for goal setting, and for supervision and evaluation.

Instruction
Levels of Performance

Indicator	Unsatisfactory	Minimum	Proficient	Evidence
Oral and Written Language	Teacher's spoken language is inaudible or written language is illegible. Spoken or written language may contain many grammar and syntax errors. Vocabulary may be inappropriate, vague, or used incorrectly, leaving students confused.	Teacher's spoken and written language is clear and correct. Vocabulary is correct but limited or is not appropriate to students' ages and backgrounds.	Teacher's spoken and written language is clear and correct. Vocabulary is appropriate to students' ages and interests.	Observation Self-Assessment
Presentation of Content	Teacher presents content in an inappropriate and unclear fashion, using poor examples.	Teacher usually presents content in an appropriate and clear fashion, linking information with students' knowledge and experience.	Teacher presents content in an appropriate and clear fashion, linking information with students' knowledge and experience. (Students contribute to the presentation of content.)	Observation Self-Assessment

FIGURE 7.3—continued
Rubric for Instruction

Indicator	Unsatisfactory	Instruction Levels of Performance Minimum	Proficient	Evidence
Questioning Techniques	Teacher's questions lack variety and are virtually all at lower levels of cognitive thinking.	Teacher's questions lack variety. Although at different levels of cognitive thinking, only some invite a response. Not adequate time for response.	Teacher consistently employs a wide variety of questions at different levels of cognitive thinking. Adequate time is available for students to respond.	Observation Self-Assessment
Discussion Techniques	Teacher mediates all questions and answers with only a few students participating and attending to class discussion.	Teacher attempts to engage students in the discussion with many students participating and attending to the class discussion.	Teacher attempts to engage all students in discussion. Students initiate relevant contributions.	Observation Self-Assessment
Response to Students	Teacher ignores or fails to respond appropriately to students' questions or interests.	Teacher attempts to accommodate students' questions or interests, with mixed results.	Teacher successfully accommodates students' questions or interests. Teacher seizes opportunities to enhance learning by building on a spontaneous event.	Observation Self-Assessment
Knowledge of Content-Related Pedagogy	Limited knowledge of pedagogical issues involved in learners attaining Vermont's Framework of Standards and Learning Opportunities.	Pedagogical knowledge present as outlined in Vermont's Learning Opportunities.	Pedagogical practices reflect some of the "best practices" stated in Vermont's Learning Opportunities.	Observation Self-Assessment

FIGURE 7.3—continued

Rubric for Instruction

		Instruction Levels of Performance			
Indicator	Unsatisfactory	Minimum	Proficient		Evidence
Grouping of Students	Instructional groups are inappropriate given students' ages or backgrounds. Students are not engaged.	Instructional groups are usually appropriate to the students and generally successful in advancing instructional goals.	Instructional groups are productive and fully appropriate to the students and the instructional goals.		Observation Self-Assessment
Persistence	Teacher either gives up or blames the student or the environment for the student's lack of success.	Teacher accepts responsibility for students' success but uses only a limited repertoire of instructional strategies.	Teacher persists in seeking effective approaches for student success, using an extensive repertoire of strategies and resources.		Observation Self-Assessment
The Developmental Characteristics of the Students	Teacher understands the developmental characteristics of children in her classes but rarely organizes classroom activities to meet developmental needs.	Teacher understands the developmental characteristics of children in her classes and sometimes sets blocks of time aside for activities that meet developmental needs (e.g., choice time twice each week).	Teacher understands the developmental characteristics of children in her classes and chooses activities that meet these needs everyday. Collaborates and consults with other teachers to meet special and exceptional needs in her classes.		Observation Self-Assessment Conference Artifacts (student work)

FIGURE 7.3—continued
Rubric for Instruction

Instruction
Levels of Performance

Indicator	Unsatisfactory	Minimum	Proficient	Evidence
Physically and Educationally Supportive Environment in Which to Teach	Classroom shows evidence of clutter and is inefficient. Classroom rules are developed by the teacher without clear student understanding (e.g., students don't feel a sense of community).	Classroom is organized and neat but changes are made infrequently (e.g., work spaces reorganized to accomplish specific activities). Classroom rules made with students but carried out inconsistently. Risk taking is inconsistent.	Equipment, work, and learning spaces maintained and organized so tasks and projects may be carried out safely, efficiently, and cooperatively.	Observation
Management of Transitions	Much time is lost during transitions.	Transitions are sporadically efficient, resulting in some unnecessary loss of instructional time.	Transitions are smooth with students assuming some responsibility for efficient operations.	Observation Self-Assessment
Management of Materials, Supplies, and Furniture	Materials, supplies, and furniture are arranged inefficiently, resulting in loss of instructional time.	Routines for handling and arranging materials, supplies, and furniture occur with little loss of instructional time.	Routines for handling and arranging materials, supplies, and furniture are seamless, with students assuming some responsibility for efficient operation.	Observation Self-Assessment

FIGURE 7.3—continued

Rubric for Instruction

| Indicator | Instruction Levels of Performance | | | Evidence |
	Unsatisfactory	Minimum	Proficient	
Performance of Noninstructional Duties	Considerable instructional time is lost in performing noninstructional duties.	Systems of performing noninstructional duties are fairly efficient, resulting in little loss of instructional time.	Systems of performing noninstructional duties are well established, with students assuming considerable responsibility for efficient operation.	Observation Self-Assessment
Structure and Pacing	The lesson has no clearly defined structure. Pacing of the lesson is too slow or too rushed.	The lesson has a clearly defined structure around which the activities are organized. Pacing of the lesson is appropriate for most students.	The lesson's structure is highly coherent, allowing for reflection and closure as appropriate for most students.	Observation Self-Assessment
Multiple Instructor Roles (e.g., direct instruction, facilitating, modeling, coaching, reflecting, guiding, observing)	Teacher generally relies on one instructor's role.	Teacher generally relies on one instructor's role and sometimes uses another one.	Instructor roles determined by the purpose of the learning and the needs of the students. Teacher demonstrates skill in multiple instructor roles.	Observation Self-Assessment Conference Portfolio

Source: Windsor Southwest Supervisory Union, 1999

Summative Evaluation

   • How do standards shape the purpose of the evaluation?

   • What are our expected roles and responsibilities in this process?

   • What is the time line for the process?

   • What are our goals? How will we know if they have been accomplished?

The revision of professional development, supervision, and evaluation in this chapter completes the overview of the components of standards linking (see Figure 1.1, p. 3). How, then, does a school or district begin implementation of the standards linking process? This will be the focus of Chapter 8.

8

Getting Started

Chances are good that you have already begun work on some aspect of the standards-linking process. Maybe you've started aligning your curriculum to state or national standards. Perhaps you are assessing student performance in relation to standards. You may be successfully implementing standards-based professional development. Now you want to start coordinating your isolated changes into a coherent, purposeful plan. This chapter offers insights and practical advice to help you achieve your goals.

Realities of Change

The power of standards linking is that piecemeal initiatives give way to focused, carefully planned strategies that are all explicitly grounded in standards. Eventually, you will align all policies, practices, resources, time, and energy of the school or district to support improved performance for all students. However, each piecemeal initiative is important to some students, staff, parents, and community members. Many initiatives have long, successful histories. Some will fit well into a revised system; others will change dramatically or disappear altogether.

Certain realities of changes hold true no matter what the work you are attempting. Some of these characteristics of change were neatly summarized by the Illinois Academy for Math and Science.

You may want to refer to this list as you encounter the inevitable challenges of linking standards:

- Things like to stay where they are.
- No object wants to move of its own accord.
- Even tiny things are reluctant to move.
- The only reason a moving object stops is that something forces it to stop.
- It takes just as much effort to stop moving as it does to start moving.
- Things like to do what they are already doing.
- Things like to keep moving in a straight line unless something forces them to change direction.
- If you always push at right angles to motion, you go in circles.
- Continuous applied force causes continuous change.
- Small forces can cause great changes in direction over time.

Five Covenants

Pathways to Education Partnerships is a collaborative that is working to enhance life expectancy and quality of life for Native Americans. Operating in northern Minnesota, the Partnership includes representatives from Native American Reservations, Tribal Colleges, the Bush Foundation, the University of Minnesota and its Extension Service, and county resource and family centers. These groups use a community planning circle to support their common goal of battling adult onset diabetes on the reservations of northern Minnesota.

Each partner makes different decisions within the Partnership's planning circle, but all partners embrace the five covenants listed in Figure 8.1. These covenants apply equally well to the process of standards linking because each school and district can make different decisions about linking standards. But these five covenants are excellent guidelines for building leadership to achieve standards-based learning.

FIGURE 8.1

The Five Covenants

The five covenants, originally developed for a collaborative effort to combat adult onset diabetes, are equally useful for building leadership to achieve standards-based learning. The covenants address norms of collaborative planning and decision-making.

• Mutual Planning
• Mutual Teaching
• Mutual Learning
• Mutual Sharing
• Mutual Participation

Source: Pathways to Education Partnerships Program, 1999, p. 3. Adapted by permission. For additional information, contact Jim Sutherland, PEP Coordinator, University of Minnesota, College of Agricultural, Food, and Environmental Sciences, 277 Coffey Hall, 1429 Eckles Ave., St. Paul, MN 55108.

Mutual Planning

The ultimate goal of standards linking is to improve all students' performances in relation to standards, however, a school or district may establish ancillary goals. For example, standards linking may be seen as a way to promote data-driven decision making, to eliminate tracking, or to address equity issues.

Your school or district must agree on these ancillary goals at the outset of planning. You also must continually monitor progress in relation to each goal throughout implementation. In this way, the goals can focus planning and help you monitor progress. These goals also form the basis for celebrating success.

Agreeing to goals may be relatively simple, but planning for their implementation is more complex. The key components of implementation are incorporated in the standards-linking overview, which is described in Figure 1.1 (p. 3). The implementation plan in Appendix B (pp. 167–173) illustrates how to establish two important elements: responsibilities and a time line.

Establishing Responsibility

The implementation plan must address responsibility at three levels: (1) Who is going to do the work? (2) Who will make certain that the work gets done? (3) Who will be responsible for quality control?

Some schools and districts adopt the "shepherd" model for implementation planning. A teacher, administrator, or community member is assigned to shepherd an aspect of implementation. The shepherd is not expected to do all of the work; rather, this person manages the workflow, monitors time lines, obtains resources, and shares results. Assigning shepherds to various aspects of the work increases ownership for implementation, builds leadership capacity, and increases the likelihood that all aspects of implementation will receive the attention they deserve.

The disadvantage of shepherding is that the work may lose coherence. The work also may be of uneven quality. This is why you must develop quality control processes from the outset. For example, all written work may flow to an editorial board, or all professional development work may flow to a local standards board. One group may review assessments for content accuracy; another group may look at the assessments' technical soundness.

In most situations, the superintendent and school board will hold the principal or curriculum director responsible for the work plan. Thus, you must clarify from the outset the degree to which the principal or curriculum director has the right to countermand work groups, shepherds, and other participants. Most people understand the need for this authority as long as the boundaries are clear at the beginning. Some schools and districts label the role of each work group's task: "input," "collaboration," or "decision." Labeling the roles helps to clarify the degree of autonomy the group enjoys and avoids the morale killer of misinterpreting roles after the fact.

Establishing a Time Line

An implementation plan also must include a clear time line for the entire implementation process. The time line should include key milestones despite the fact that it will change—the work will almost certainly take longer than anticipated. However, a time line provides clear deadlines to work groups, shepherds, and administrators. The time line also provides a tool to track progress and shift resources along the way.

The work of standards linking is interdependent, therefore work groups should not adjust time lines independently. If a subgroup needs more time or resources, decisions must be made by the whole work team, weighing the needs of the subgroup and the effects on the entire system. Once a decision to adjust time lines is made, the entire plan must be modified so that the work retains its flow.

Mutual Teaching and Mutual Learning

Implementation of standards linking requires knowledge and experience in multiple areas. This includes knowledge of the standards, content-area expertise, experience with instructional strategies, technical expertise in assessment and data analysis, and experience in systems planning. No participant is likely to have expertise and experience in all areas. Therefore, implementation of standards linking requires mutual covenants of teaching and learning.

As you develop a time line and assign responsibilities, create a teaching and learning plan. The plan will evolve over time as the process yields new questions to research and fresh areas to explore. In terms of learning, remember that different levels of expertise are needed for implementation to occur. Consider a clock: We all need to know how to tell time, but we all don't need to know how the springs, wheels, or quartz movements operate behind the face of the clock. With standards linking, all participants need to know the goals, but not all participants need to know the specifics involved in implementing each area of the plan.

Using assessment as an example, here are the different levels of expertise that the Lamoille North Supervisory Unit, Morrisville, Vermont, identified:

- **Practitioner:** Requires ability to implement the assessment in the classroom, to obtain and analyze results, to communicate results to students and parents, and to use results to make instructional decisions in the classroom.
- **Student and Parent:** Requires ability to understand what results indicate in terms of student performance and what needs to be done to improve performance.
- **Item Developer:** Requires deep understanding of the standards to be assessed, related content, and protocols for developing assessment items.
- **Assessment Tool Developer:** Requires understanding of the process of developing assessment tools, such as field-testing, piloting, benchmarking, and scaling. Also requires understanding of issues related to reliability and validity.
- **Assessment Tool Selector:** Requires understanding and application of criteria for standards-based assessments.
- **Developer of Comprehensive Assessment Plan:** Requires

understanding of strengths and weaknesses of all assessments in the system and ways assessments work together to measure student performance in relation to the standards. Requires identifying needs for additional assessments and setting priorities for their development or selection.

As participants identify their roles and responsibilities in standards linking, they simultaneously serve as learners and teachers. The learner role includes becoming familiar with research and best practices, contributing to product development, and learning from other team members. The teacher role includes sharing learning with others. Here is an example of how these roles play out, again related to assessment.

> In a high school, part of the standards-linking plan calls for development of standards-based end-of-course assessments. Two science teachers and the curriculum coordinator are assigned to this process, with the curriculum coordinator as shepherd.

> As learners, they conduct research and locate standards-based assessments for chemistry and physics developed by other high schools. They test these assessments, review data related to their reliability, and measure them against their locally adopted criteria for assessments. They decide to recommend adoption of these assessments. As teachers, it is their responsibility to teach the others involved in planning how these assessments fit into the comprehensive assessment plan. They are also responsible for working with colleagues to implement these assessments and build a system for reporting results to students, parents, and the community.

> Because they cannot locate end-of-course assessments for their integrated science program in grades 9 and 10, they must develop these assessments. They work with colleagues to create standards-based performance tasks and to develop scoring rubrics. They then work with an assessment expert to field test,

pilot, and benchmark the assessments. Once this process is complete, they work with colleagues through implementation issues.

Mutual Sharing

The implementation of standards linking plays a key role in building a learning community within a school or district because all participants act both as teachers and learners. No one has all the needed information for the work, and all participants have the responsibility to learn and to share their learning. Mutual sharing is the fourth of the five covenants, but it is one of the most important. Implementation of standards linking will not succeed without a commitment to mutual sharing.

Mutual sharing is achieved through both formal and informal communication. One school district offers a standards-linking update for its school board on a quarterly basis. The school board meetings are broadcast over a public access channel, therefore this update serves as a vehicle for communicating with the community. Schools often use traditional forms of communication such as newsletters, annual reports, and staff meetings to communicate progress. Some schools post information on their Web sites. Building on the participatory nature of planning, many schools also use community forums and focus groups.

One key communication challenge is to continually frame progress in terms of the big picture. Standards linking is complex, and everyone involved must examine and reexamine how all the pieces fit together. If this is not done repeatedly for all participants, the power of the systems approach becomes lost in implementation.

Figure 8.2 shows an example of a communication plan. This example, drawn from the work of the Washington Central Supervisory Union, would fit well into a broader, overall communications plan.

Mutual Participation

The final covenant is mutual participation because standards linking profoundly affects everyone in the learning community. The level of participation varies according to a person's role, circumstance, and competing priorities, but all members of the learning community must be part of the process.

Participation of the broader community increases as members see ways they can directly support implementation. For example, in some communities, businesses commit to carefully examine standards-linked transcripts in the hiring process. Some (but not enough) colleges and universities are committing to development of K–16 standards and are increasing the importance of standards-based performance in admissions decisions. Human service agencies, corrections departments, and school communities are collecting data with the family or individual as the unit of analysis. They then can share and combine data to inform comprehensive delivery of services, reducing confusion, and fragmentation. Standards linking yields data clearly tied to explicit standards and can serve as a catalyst for developing these types of community initiatives.

Student and parental participation increases as they see how the process affects children. Increased participation is one reason that alignment of the reporting system (including report cards, transcripts, and parent conferences) is a significant step in the transformation to a standards-linking system.

Staff members have seen many educational innovations come and go. Thus, they may at first opt out of standards linking. In our experience, when staff members see that the process affects both the classroom and student performance—and that it assigns clear responsibility for standards to both teachers and students—they quickly become active participants, and even leaders, in implementation.

FIGURE 8.2

Sample Communication Plan

This sample communication plan, developed by a school district to guide its communication of standards linking, can serve as a guideline as you develop your own plan.

Who Needs to Know?	What Do They Need to Know?	Who Will Tell Them?	How Will They Be Informed?	By When?
Students, parents, community, businesses, higher education, staff, policy makers	Importance of standards-based assessment	Standards Linking Leadership and Assessment Work Group, superintendent, curriculum leaders, principals, teachers	Newsletter, Web page, board presentations, community forums, classroom discussion, staff meetings, parent conferences.	Ongoing
Planning groups, students, parents, community, businesses, higher education, staff, policy makers	Connections among standards-based assessment and other aspects of standards-linking	Standards Linking Leadership and Work Groups, superintendent, curriculum leaders, principals, teachers	Newsletter, Web page, board presentations, community forums, classroom discussion, staff meetings	Ongoing
Planning groups, students, parents, community, businesses, higher education, staff, policy makers, colleagues in other schools and districts, state department of education	Process of adoption or creation of standards-based performance assessments	Assessment Work Group, curriculum leaders, principals, teachers	Newsletter, Web page, classroom discussion, staff meetings, parent conferences	As implemented

FIGURE 8.2—continued

Sample Communication Plan

Who Needs to Know?	What Do They Need to Know?	Who Will Tell Them?	How Will They Be Informed?	By When?
Planning groups, students, parents, community, businesses, higher education, staff, policy makers, state department of education	Reporting of results	Superintendent, curriculum leaders, principals, teachers	Newsletter, Web page, classroom discussion, staff meetings, parent conferences, report cards, transcripts, state reports, newspaper	As available
Planning groups, students, parents, community, businesses, higher education, staff, policy makers, state department of education	Use of results in action planning	Action Planning teams, superintendent, curriculum leaders, principals, teachers	Action plans, newsletter, Web page, classroom discussion, staff meetings, parent conferences, state reports	Annually

Source: Washington Central Supervisory Union

Mutual participation includes actively celebrating successes. Celebrate milestones such as completing assignment of standards, developing the comprehensive assessment system, and completing your first standards-based action plan. As implementation continues, the focus of celebration moves to enhanced student learning. Graduation challenges, inquiry fairs, and other culminating activities provide opportunities to showcase student performance in relation to standards. As the comprehensive assessment plan yields evidence of student learning in relation to standards, a schoolwide or communitywide celebration of student success provides the chance to share powerful testimonies of standards-based learning.

The action plan is also a celebration in that it clearly states a mutual commitment to continued growth.

Although the efforts needed to implement a standards-linking system are great, so are the rewards. Celebrating student learning is the most fundamental, most motivating, and most powerful affirmation for the learning community. Celebration of progress and success provides the impetus for continuous systems-based improvement.

Appendix A

Learning Opportunity Survey for Teachers

This Learning Opportunity Survey for teachers can be used to gain important information related to teacher preparation, classroom practice, and professional development.

Part 1: General Background
Please write in or circle the most appropriate answer for each question.
1. What is the name of your school?

2. What is your gender?

3. Which description best describes you?

__ African or African
   American
__ Asian or Asian American
__ Hispanic or Latino
__ White, not of Hispanic
   origin

__ American Indian or
   Alaskan Native
__ Filipino or Filipino American
__ Pacific Islander
__ Multiethnic or biracial

4. Counting this year, how many years in total (include part-time teaching) have you taught at either the elementary or secondary level?

__ 2 years or less
__ 11–24 years

__ 3–5 years
__ 25 years or more

__ 6–10 years

5. Counting this year, how many years in total have you taught the following subjects? (Include permanent, full-time, and part-time assignments, but not substitute assignments.)

	2 years or less	3–5 years	6–10 years	11–24 years	25 years or more
Reading	——	——	——	——	——
Writing	——	——	——	——	——
Language Arts	——	——	——	——	——
Mathematics	——	——	——	——	——
Science	——	——	——	——	——
History	——	——	——	——	——
Social Studies	——	——	——	——	——
Civics	——	——	——	——	——

6. What level of education do you have for each of the following areas?

	Less than a minor in a bachelor's degree	Bachelor's degree minor	Bachelor's degree (major)	Master's degree	Doctorate
Mathematics	——	——	——	——	——
Science	——	——	——	——	——
Education	——	——	——	——	——
English	——	——	——	——	——
Social Science	——	——	——	——	——
Psychology	——	——	——	——	——
Other	——	——	——	——	——

7. In which of the following areas do you have 18 or more credits?

Mathematics	——
Science	——
Education	——
English	——
Social Sciences	——

8. During the last five years, how often have you taken courses or participated in professional development activities in the following areas?

	Not at all	Once	Two or more times	Ongoing participation
Reading or reading education	___	___	___	___
Writing or writing education	___	___	___	___
Mathematics or mathematics education	___	___	___	___
Science or science education	___	___	___	___
Use of telecommunications	___	___	___	___
Use of technology such as computers	___	___	___	___
Cooperative group instruction	___	___	___	___
Interdisciplinary instruction	___	___	___	___
Assessment by portfolios	___	___	___	___
Performance-based assessment	___	___	___	___
Teaching higher-order thinking skills	___	___	___	___
Teaching students from different cultural backgrounds	___	___	___	___
Teaching students with special needs (e.g., visually impaired, gifted and talented)	___	___	___	___
Teaching Limited English Proficient students	___	___	___	___
Classroom management and organization	___	___	___	___
Other professional issues	___	___	___	___

9. Which of the following statements is true about how well your school system provides you with the instructional materials and other resources you need to teach your class?

___ I get all the resources I need.   ___ I get most of the resources I need.
___ I get some of the resources I need.   ___ I don't get any of the resources I need.

10. Is there a curriculum specialist available to help or advise you in the following areas?

	Yes	No
Mathematics	___	___
Science	___	___
Reading	___	___
Writing	___	___

11. How many school hours do you have designated as preparation time per week?

__ None   __ Less than 1   __ 1–2   __ 3–4   __ 5   __ More than 5

12. Which best describes your current school setting?

__ Urban   __ Suburban   __ Rural

Part 2: Mathematics Preparation
1. How well prepared do you feel you are in each of the following topics or areas?

	Very well prepared	Prepared	Somewhat prepared	Not well prepared
Methods of teaching elementary mathematics	___	___	___	___
Number systems and numeration	___	___	___	___
Measurement in mathematics	___	___	___	___
Geometry	___	___	___	___
Probability/statistics	___	___	___	___
Patterns, functions, and algebra	___	___	___	___
Calculus	___	___	___	___
Abstract/linear algebra	___	___	___	___
Estimation	___	___	___	___
Problem solving in mathematics	___	___	___	___
Use of manipulatives (e.g., counting blocks or geometric shapes) in mathematics instruction	___	___	___	___
Use of calculators in mathematics instruction	___	___	___	___
Using mathematics portfolios	___	___	___	___
Using the Mathematics Portfolio Scoring Guide	___	___	___	___
Understanding students' thinking about mathematics	___	___	___	___
Gender issues in the teaching of mathematics	___	___	___	___
Teaching students from different cultural backgrounds	___	___	___	___

2. Which one or two of the following statements best represents the alignment of your instructional planning and delivery and the Vermont Framework of Standards and Learning Opportunities for mathematics? Mark no more than two of the following statements.

__ I use a curriculum or program that was chosen based on the standards
__ I use a curriculum or program that was reviewed for alignment with the standards
__ I have created and used one or more standards based units of study in mathematics
__ I have used one or more standards based units of study in mathematics
__ I have changed or written one or more mathematics lesson plans to incorporate the standards
__ I have not had time yet to work with the standards in mathematics
__ I am waiting for my school or supervisor to provide guidance and materials

3. Which of the following programs, textbooks, or materials do you use as your primary, secondary, or supplemental source for your instructional program? Check only one in each column

	Primary Source	Secondary Source	Supplemental Source
Connected Mathematics	___	___	___
Interactive Mathematics	___	___	___
Interactive Math, Science and Technology	___	___	___
Mathematics in Context	___	___	___
MathThematics	___	___	___
Mathscape: Seeing, Thinking Math	___	___	___
Textbooks by Saxon	___	___	___
Textbooks by Addison-Wesley	___	___	___
Textbooks by D. C. Heath	___	___	___
Textbooks by Scott Foresman	___	___	___
Other Textbooks	___	___	___
Transitions (UCSMP)	___	___	___
Visual Math	___	___	___
Resource Books such as those by Marilyn Burns and Creative Publications	___	___	___
Teacher Developed Materials	___	___	___
Other	___	___	___

4. How many years have you been using the primary source noted in question 3?

___ This is the first year ___ This is the second year
___ This is the third year ___ Four years or more

5. How much time have you spent in professional development to prepare for using or implementing the primary source mentioned? Include attendance at professional meetings and conferences, workshops, and seminars.

___ None ___ Less than 6 hours ___ 6–15 hours ___ 16–35 hours
___ 36–55 hours ___ More than 55 hours ___ Not applicable

6. The above professional development adequately prepared and supported me in implementing the mathematics program that is my primary source.

___ Strongly Agree ___ Agree ___ Undecided ___ Disagree ___ Strongly Disagree
___ Not Applicable

Part 3: Mathematics Instructional Information
In answering the following questions, please base your answers on one course that you teach whose participants are predominantly 8th graders.

1. The class is

___ Algebra I ___ Grade 8 Mathematics ___ General Mathematics
___ Geometry ___ Integrated Mathematics 1 ___ PreCalculus ___ Statistics

2. How much time do you spend each week on mathematics instruction with this class?

___ 2 ½ hours or less ___ More than 2½ hours, but less than 4 hours ___ 4 hours or more

3. Approximately how much mathematics homework do you assign to students in this class each day?

___ None ___ 15 minutes ___ 30 minutes ___ 45 minutes
___ One hour ___ More than one hour

4. Which best describes the availability of computers for use by students in your mathematics class?

__ None available
__ One within the classroom
__ Two or three within the classroom
__ Four or more within the classroom
__ Available in a computer laboratory, but difficult to access or schedule
__ Available in a computer laboratory; easy to access or schedule

5. If you do use computers, what is the primary use of these computers for mathematics instruction?

__ Drill and practice
__ Demonstration of new topics in mathematics
__ Playing mathematical/learning games
__ Simulations and applications
__ I do not use computers for instruction

6. Do the students in this class have access to calculators owned by the school?

__ Yes   __ No

7. Do you provide instruction to students in this class in the use of calculators?

__ Yes   __ No

8. In your mathematics instruction, how important do you consider each of the following to be? Check one column for each statement.

	Very Important	Somewhat Important	Not Very Important	Not Important
Involving students in constructing and applying mathematical ideas	____	____	____	____
Using problem solving both as a goal of instruction and as a means of investigating important mathematical concepts	____	____	____	____
Using questioning techniques that promote student interaction and discussion	____	____	____	____

	Very Important	Somewhat Important	Not Very Important	Not Important
Using the results of classroom assessments to inform instructional decisions	___	___	___	___
Using the Vermont Mathematics Scoring Guide to provide feedback to students	___	___	___	___

9. On average, for each of the mathematics class periods you teach, how many students are in a class?

__ 1–10 students   __ 11–20 students   __ 21–25 students   __ 26–30 students
__ 31–35 students   __ 36 or more students

10. In total, about how many students do you prepare for each day?

__ 10 or fewer   __ 11–25   __ 26–35   __ 36–50   __ 51 or more

11. How often do the students in this class do each of the following?

	Almost Every Day	Once or Twice a Week	Once or Twice a Month	Never or Hardly Ever
Do mathematics problems from their textbooks	___	___	___	___
Do mathematics problems on worksheets	___	___	___	___
Solve mathematics problems in small groups or with a partner	___	___	___	___
Work with objects like rulers	___	___	___	___
Work with counting blocks or geometric shapes	___	___	___	___
Use a calculator	___	___	___	___
Use the mathematics scoring guide/rubric to evaluate their own or another student's work	___	___	___	___
Take mathematics tests	___	___	___	___
Write a few sentences about how to solve a mathematics problem	___	___	___	___

	Almost Every Day	Once or Twice a Week	Once or Twice a Month	Never or Hardly Ever
Talk to the class about mathematics work	___	___	___	___
Write reports or do mathematics projects	___	___	___	___
Discuss solutions to mathematics problems with other students	___	___	___	___
Work and discuss mathematics problems that reflect real-life situations	___	___	___	___
Do work that goes into their mathematics portfolios	___	___	___	___
Use a computer	___	___	___	___
Talk with you about their mathematics work using the Mathematics Portfolio Scoring Guide	___	___	___	___

12. In this mathematics class, how often do you address each of the following?

	A Lot	Some	A Little	None
Numbers and operations	___	___	___	___
Measurement	___	___	___	___
Geometry	___	___	___	___
Data analysis, statistics, and probability (informal introduction of concepts)	___	___	___	___
Algebra and functions (informal introduction of concepts)	___	___	___	___
Learning mathematics facts and concepts	___	___	___	___
Learning skills and procedures needed to solve routine problems	___	___	___	___
Developing reasoning and analytical ability to solve unique problems	___	___	___	___
Learning how to communicate ideas in mathematics effectively	___	___	___	___

13. How many years have you used the mathematics portfolio program instructionally with students?

__ None   __ One year   __ Two years   __ Three years   __ Four or more years

14. How much do you agree with each of the following statements?

	Strongly Agree	Agree	Undecided	Disagree	Strongly Disagree	Not Applicable
Using the Vermont Portfolio program and scoring guide has strengthened **my own** content knowledge of mathematics	____	____	____	____	____	____
Using the Vermont Portfolio program and scoring guide has strengthened **my students'** content knowledge of mathematics	____	____	____	____	____	____
Using the Vermont Portfolio program and scoring guide has strengthened **my students'** complex problem solving abilities	____	____	____	____	____	____

Source: Vermont Department of Education, 1999

Appendix B

Sample School District Plan for Linking Standards to the Curriculum, K–12

The following is a standards-linking curriculum and assessment implementation plan and budget for schools from kindergarten through 12th grade.

ACTION STEP	WHAT	WHEN	WHO	DECISION POINTS	COST/SOURCE OF FUNDS
Complete plan with budget	A combined curriculum and implementation plan with budget.	May 2000	Peg & Robbe with administrative vote.	Decide to proceed	As broken down below
Creating the database					
1. Revise, if necessary, the software for the database and put on computers.	The database comes ready to fill in. There just needs to be a review to see if any standards particular to WCSU are added.	Dennis: May 2000 (5th and 6th grade teacher will work at U32) SU Tech support: August 2000	Dennis at the high school and middle level; the SU tech person at the elementary schools.	Decide where standards-linking group will have access to computers, which computers will have installation	

Appendix B—continued

ACTION STEP	WHAT	WHEN	WHO	DECISION POINTS	COST/SOURCE OF FUNDS
2. Appoint standards-linking team.	A six-member team to create the recommendations and oversee the entry of data into database.	May: High School and Middle Level August: K–4	U32 HS & Middle Level: David & Peg K–4: Curriculum Coordinator and Standards-Linking Elementary Coordinator	Decide which members will be responsible for which recommendations 7–12	Approximately $15,000 for teacher stipends:11 days @ $150 per day for 7 member team including food Goals 2000 K–4 $13,650
3. Go over existing materials that are ready to be entered in the database.	Use existing maps done by high school departments and prepare them to be entered into database.	May: 9–12 July: 5–8 September: K–4	Standards-Linking Team & Curriculum Coordinator	Look at maps and make sure they have correct information for data entry	
4. Hire support staff to enter existing data.	Use the above maps and enter data.	May/June: 9–12 June/July: 5–8 August/Sept.: K–4	Standards-Linking Team and support staff	Decide what data goes where and enter it	Four staff at approx. $15 an hour, 8 hours, three days = $1,500 Title 2
5. Train people in the use of the database.	File-maker Pro is the software that will be used to create the database. Training should occur so the designated staff can enter data.	May: 9–12 June: 5–8 August: K–4	Dennis and Staff at U32 5–12 August/ September K–4		Part of stipend

Appendix B—continued

ACTION STEP	WHAT	WHEN	WHO	DECISION POINTS	COST/SOURCE OF FUNDS
6. Team starts to sort and make recommendations around standards that are not assigned to any grade or course (e.g., Vital Results).	The remaining standards are assigned to courses, grades, departments by standards-linking team; data is entered into database.	Grades 9–12: July 5, 6, 7	High School Standards-Linking Team	Which of the remaining standards are taught and where are they assessed	Part of stipend mentioned in number 2
7. Middle-level team coordinates standards taught by unit and themes.	Middle-level team reviews the curriculum work at 5–6 and begins to designate by theme and units the standards that will be taught and assessed across teams.	June 21, 22, 23	8-member team	Which standards will be taught and assessed across the three teams in which grades	8 staff at $150 for 3 days; $4,500 including stipends and food Goals 2000
8. Team starts to sort and make recommendations around standards that are not assigned to any grade or course (e.g., Vital Results).	Team takes the work from June and the remaining standards are assigned to courses, grades, departments by recommendation of standards-linking team; data is entered into database.	Grades 5–12: July 12, 13, 14, 26 Grades K–4 to be arranged in fall	Standards-Linking Team 5–8 and Curriculum Coordinator—7 person team, one from each building and 2 from 7 & 8 grade teachers	Full framework, which standards are taught and assessed where	$150 per day, 11 days, for 7 staff $12,000 including food Goals 2000 and Title II
9. Work is assessed by standards-linking coordinator and superintendent.	The 5–12 draft of work is reviewed by Robbe.	Grades 5–12: August 1 Grades K–4: TBA	Curriculum Coordinators and Standards-Linking Coordinators	Check and discuss progress of work	$1,500: $500 stipend for each of 3 coordinators Title II

Appendix B—continued

ACTION STEP	WHAT	WHEN	WHO	DECISION POINTS	COST/SOURCE OF FUNDS
Create Student Assessment Profile	A 5–12 student assessment profile that shows which standards are to be assessed and tracked throughout high school.	August 2, 3, 16, 17, 22 K–4 TBA	Full Standards-Linking Team grades 5–12, Curriculum Coordinator	Which standards will be taught, assessed, communicated throughout the career of a student	Stipends already included, $500 for food Title VI
1. Create a process/criteria that would define the standards that need to be tracked across the student's career.	The process enables people to determine the standards that will be tracked.	See Above	Full Standards-Linking Team grades 5–12	See Above	Included in Above
2. Create a process to define which evidence should be tracked across the student's career.	See Above	See Above	See Above	See Above	Included in Above
3. Define the profile.	Standards-based rubrics, checklists, short answer, assessment that will be used across the SU matched to the standards that are determined to be tracked across the student's career.	See Above	See Above	See Above	See Above

Appendix B—continued

ACTION STEP	WHAT	WHEN	WHO	DECISION POINTS	COST/SOURCE OF FUNDS
4. Create a feedback loop so that there is rich feedback and consensus building along the ways as standards and evidence are being determined.	Surveys, forums, department discussions that allow teachers to understand and see the implications of assessing students across a common set of standards and letting them determine if the standards chosen are appropriate.	See Above	See Above	See Above	See Above
5. Add profile to comprehensive assessment plan.	Take the existing comprehensive assessment and complete by adding the assessments of the profile.	5–12 Between August 3rd and 16th K–4 TBA	Curriculum Coordinator	See Above	See Above
6. Present comprehensive assessment draft and get feedback, discussion, and implications from principals.	This is the first opportunity that administration can review and give feedback to work done to date.	5–12: August 11 at Admin. Retreat K–4: TBA	Standards-Linking Coordinators, Principals, Superintendents, and Curriculum Coordinator	Implications for starting the work in K–6, professional development, impact on instruction	Work already allocated
7. Present full draft to administrators at first administrative meeting.	Continued discussion including policy implications.	5–12: August 15 K–4: TBA	Standards-Linking Coordinators and Admin. Team	Review and support for the comprehensive assessment plan and the assessment profile	Already budgeted

Appendix B—continued

ACTION STEP	WHAT	WHEN	WHO	DECISION POINTS	COST/SOURCE OF FUNDS
8. Get full faculty feedback on draft assessment profile.	Surveys, forums, department discussions that allow teachers to understand and see the implications of assessing students across a common set of standards and letting them determine if the standards chosen are appropriate.	5–12: August 29 K–4: TBA	Standards-Linking Team and Curriculum Coordinator with support from building principal.	Feedback that will be incorporated in draft 2	No additional expense
9. Hold an inservice training meeting dedicated to assessment.	A day to learn about embedded assessment that results in assessing students as they demonstrate the evidence as related to the standard.	Aug. 30 All staff	Curriculum Coordinator and consultants		No additional expense
10. Create draft 2 of assessment profile and comprehensive assessment.	The feedback from the teachers will be sorted, and a set of recommendations will emerge and be incorporated into draft 2.	October 2000	Curriculum Coordinator and Standards-Linking Team 5–12 TBA grade K–4	Changes in plan and profile must be decided on	No additional expense

Appendix B—continued

ACTION STEP	WHAT	WHEN	WHO	DECISION POINTS	COST/SOURCE OF FUNDS
11. Ongoing professional development in embedding assessments into classrooms.	With the emergence of the profile, teachers need to learn how to embed the assessments into their daily practice.	October 2000 with emphasis as institute summer of 2001. A week for each level.	Curriculum Coordinator and others	Which assessments to start incorporating (e.g., writing and problem solving rubric) but in the summer work to integrate more	Goal 2000 grant or CFG 2002
12. Begin integrating. Assessment profile integrated into class and course instruction.	Standards-based instruction incorporated; all assessment needed for assessment profile.	Fall 2001	Curriculum Coordinator, staff, and other supports		
13. Student work is reviewed and used for instructional conversations	Discussions of what is appropriate demonstration of evidence as related to standards, what areas of content do general students acquire, where are students not meeting the standards, are there areas of transition, 6–7, 7–9 that need to be analyzed.	Fall 2001	Staff	Areas in need of further data, areas where identification of at-risk students must be tightened, issues of instruction are discussed and decided by staff	

Source: Washington Central Supervisory Union, Vermont

Glossary

action plan A school's program for improving student performance. Includes analysis of relevant data, identification of needs, clear goals and tasks, and roles and responsibilities.

alignment The directness of the link among standards, local curriculum, instructional materials, instructional methods, and assessments.

all students The population to which standards are applicable. A small percent of students may not meet the standards because of the extreme severity of their disabilities (e.g., a severely disabled high school student who functions at a preschool academic level). Accommodations for such students should be specifically addressed in their individualized educational programs within the spirit and context of what the standards intend. The definition of *all students* includes specifically the following:

- Students who have been denied access in any way to educational opportunity, as well as those who have not.
- Students who are female, as well as those who are male.
- Students who are African-American, Hispanic, Asian, Native American, or members of other minorities, as well as those who are members of the racial or ethnic minority.
- Students who are socioeconomically disadvantaged, as well as those who are more advantaged.
- Students who have not been successful in school, as well as those who have been successful. (Adapted from the National Council of Teachers of Mathematics, 1989).

analytic scoring A procedure in which performances are evaluated for selected dimensions or traits, with each trait receiving a separate score. Analytic scoring involves a quantitative judgment that identified dimensions or traits are more or less present. Analytic scoring reports a profile of characteristics or attributes. Analytic scoring guides specify criteria to be assessed, provide a separate score for each criterion, and may include a composite score for overall performance. In some cases, the composite score is weighted based on the importance of each dimension.

anchor Another word for benchmark.

assessment The process of quantifying, describing, gathering data about, or giving feedback about performance. Assessment results are used to identify instructional practices that should be improved, to focus professional development for teachers, and to supply new or different instructional resources for learners.

assessment plan A set of choices regarding how student learning will be assessed in relation to identified standards and criteria.

authentic assessment The process of gathering evidence and documentation of a student's learning and growth in ways that resemble "real life" as closely as possible (e.g., a driving test, a presentation to a board on a "real" issue). To measure growth and progress, students' work is compared to their previous work rather than to the work of others. Authentic assessment is based on what the child actually does in a variety of contexts at points throughout the school year. Authentic work represents the student's application, not mere acquisition, of knowledge and skills. Authentic assessment also engages students in the activity and reflects best instructional activities.

baseline data Data collected first to establish the starting point from which we can measure change.

benchmark An actual example of student work that provides an interpretation of a performance standard according to age, grade, or developmental levels. Benchmark can refer to samples of student work that illustrate excellent or adequate performance. Benchmark also can refer to reachable targets at various grade levels or ages. Benchmark is a synonym for anchor.

bias The act of employing language, process, or structure that has different meanings for; is emotionally loaded for; reinforces stereotypes about; or does not encompass the full range of race, gender, ethnicity, age, sexual orientation, or physical or mental condition.

classroom assessment Evaluations that are ongoing and relevant to immediate learning. Classroom assessment is embedded in learning and teaching activities and is an integral part of instruction.

close-ended tasks Tasks that have one right or best answer. Close-ended tasks should only be used to assess specific knowledge or information students have acquired.

comprehensive assessment system The tools and processes used to gather data about student results, the implementation of programs and practices, and the resources necessary to support student learning in relation to standards. Once data are gathered, they are used to make decisions about program improvement.

constructed response items or tasks Those items or tasks for which students must create a response or answer (e.g., a written or oral answer, a product, or a performance). Constructed response items or tasks are used to assess processes or procedural knowledge or to probe for students' understanding of knowledge and information.

Constructed response tasks are often contrasted with selected response items or tasks.

context The circumstances in which a performance is embedded. For example, problem solving can be assessed in the context of a specific subject or in the context of a real-life laboratory problem requiring the use of mathematical, scientific, and communication skills. Science process skills can be assessed in the context of a large-scale, high-stakes assessment or in the context of a classroom test. Context can also distinguish whether a performance is completed on demand or over time. Finally, context can refer to whether a task is done alone, in pairs, or in a group.

criteria The dimensions or characteristics of standards used to judge student work. When combined with a scale and performance descriptions, these elements valued in student performance become rubrics or scoring guides to be used in assessment. Scoring guides embody and express criteria. For example, criteria for good reading might include characteristics such as fluency, flexibility, making connections within and between texts, and making connections with personal experience. These criteria would be expressed in rubrics, and the rubrics used to assess students' reading performance. Benchmark papers or performances may be used to identify each level of proficiency in the scoring guide.

criterion-referenced assessment Assessment that compares a student's performance according to a description of the desired performance. For example: She typed 55 words per minute without errors when the criterion was 40 words a minute with no more than two errors. All standards-based assessments are criterion-referenced assessments, though not all criterion-referenced assessments are standards-based assessments. Criterion-referenced assessment is often contrasted with norm-referenced assessment.

data Records and reports of formal and informal observations, experiences, and events. Data are facts or figures from which conclusions may be drawn. Data become information when they are put to use, as for planning and decision making.

diagnostic assessment Assessment that enables one to infer what a student does and does not know and is and is not able to do.

disaggregated data Data that analyzes student performance by demographic groups (e.g., males vs. females, low socioeconomic group vs. high socioeconomic group). Disaggregation means knowing about the performance of whole groups versus subgroups.

evaluation Judgment regarding the quality, value, or worth of a response, product, or performance based on established criteria. Evaluations are usually based on multiple sources of information. The terms "evaluation" and "assessment" are often used interchangeably.

exemplars Benchmark papers or performances. Exemplars provide a clear and stable reference point for giving feedback to students, educators, and the public in relation to standards. Exemplars give students a clear picture of the targets they are aiming for; and they define levels of performance in concrete, meaningful, and public ways.

formative assessment Ongoing assessment providing data to guide instruction and improve performance.

generalizability A term that refers to the extent to which the performances sampled by a set of assessment items or tasks are representative of the broader domain being assessed. For example, can generalizations about a student's problem-solving ability be made from the student's performance on a specific set of 10 problem-solving tasks? How many samples of student work are needed to be confident that a student can problem solve in mathematics?

generalized rubric A scoring methodology that can be used for a wide range of products and performances and multiple tasks to which the same criteria can be applied. For example, generalized rubrics are often used to assess standards for problem solving, communication, and scientific method.

holistic scoring The process of assigning one score to a performance based on overall quality. Using a holistic scoring guide, performance is judged qualitatively by a single description for each level on the scale. Holistic scoring is appropriate when a dimension or attribute cannot be broken down into separate components or criteria, such as creativity, fitness, or teamwork. Holistic scoring is also used when clumping of the characteristics of a performance on a standard is the more useful level of information, such as the overall quality of a piece of writing.

indicator A measure that describes performance related to standards and other aspects of educational systems. An indicator must have a common, agreed upon, consistent definition and a reference point or standard against which performance can be judged. An indicator must meet technical standards of quality, such as measuring what is intended to be measured (validity) and measuring consistently (reliability).

item bias The degree to which the score on a test item is related to race, gender, ethnicity, age, sexual orientation, or physical or mental condition of the respondent as well as to any difference in the construct being assessed.

large-scale assessment Assessment done for purposes and audiences beyond the classroom. Large-scale assessments are usually standardized to some extent and given to large numbers of students.

learning opportunities Recommended practices to support all students in attaining the standards. These are presented for access, instruction, assessment, connections, and best practices in the fields of knowledge; represent areas that can be influenced by the teacher; and are supported by current research and best practices.

multiple measures Evaluations that provide more than one way for students to demonstrate attainment of a standard. Students need to be provided with multiple opportunities to perform in relation to standards. Multiple opportunities to perform can apply to the assessment approach (open-ended vs. close-ended), format (constructed response vs. selected response), or context (on demand vs. over time, the setting, the purpose of the assessment).

multiscoring A simultaneous or sequential approach to scoring that provides scores for more than one standard from one task.

norm-referenced assessment Assessments designed to compare the performance of an individual student or group to another student or group by distributing performance across a normal curve and in which not all students assessed can perform at the highest level. For example: She typed better than 80 percent of her classmates. This type of assessment is frequently contrasted with criterion-referenced assessment.

on-demand assessment Assessment that takes place at a predetermined time and place. On-demand refers to a performance that is done at a point in time and over a limited amount of time. The task must be doable in the time provided. The response is an ad hoc performance, usually a rough or interim draft. State tests, SATs, and most final exams are examples of on-demand assessment.

open-ended task A performance task with no single correct response. Open-ended tasks are used to determine how students use what they know, how they demonstrate a skill or process, how they communicate what they understand, or how they apply what they know in a new context.

over time Refers to a performance that is done over an extended period of time and usually revisited several times, resulting in an evolved or final draft. Problem solving that truly involves the "unraveling" of an issue or circumstance must be done over time.

performance assessment Direct observation and judgment of student products or performances. Good-quality performance assessment has preestablished performance criteria. In standards-based assessment, these criteria are taken directly from the standards.

performance standard An established level of achievement, quality of performance, or degree of proficiency on a standard. This is determined based on multiple performances. A performance standard is usually set by an expert group on the basis of the standard, student performance data, knowledge of what students are capable of doing, and the intended use of the results.

portfolio A purposeful, integrated collection of student work showing effort, progress, or achievement in one or more areas. Usefulness for instruction and assessment is enhanced when students select the items for their portfolios, self-reflection is encouraged, and criteria for success are clear.

primary trait scoring A scoring procedure by which products or performances are evaluated by limiting attention to a single aspect or a few selected aspects of a criterion. It focuses on one or two specific attributes or characteristics and acts like a checklist. For example, if a student is asked to write to the Department of Energy to urge the opening or closing of a nuclear plant, the primary traits might be using the correct form of address and the correct letter form. Scorers would attend to only these two traits.

proficiency Having or demonstrating an expected degree of knowledge or skill in a particular area.

prompt An assignment or directions asking students to undertake a task or series of tasks. Complete prompts present the context of the situation, the problems to be solved, and the criteria by which the responses will be evaluated.

reliability The degree to which the results of an assessment are dependable and yield consistent results. Reliability is an indication of the consistency of scores across evaluators, across time, or across different tasks that measure the same thing. An assessment is considered reliable to the degree the same responses receive the same scores no matter when the assessment occurs or who does the scoring. Reliability is a statistical term that defines the extent to which errors of measurement are absent from an assessment instrument. The following issues are particularly relevant to establishing reliability:

• Criteria that are clear, do not overlap, and are taken directly from standards.
• A scale that makes clear distinctions among its levels.
• Performance descriptions that are specific, observable, and can be documented.
• Exemplars of student work that illustrate levels of attainment.
• Evidence of consistent judgment over time and across students.

rubric An established set of parameters for scoring or rating students' performance on tasks. Good rubrics consist of a fixed measurement scale (e.g., 4-point), a set of clear criteria, performance descriptions for each criterion at each point on the scale, and sample responses (anchors) that illustrate various levels of performance.

sampling The selection of an array of performances to be assessed that is wide enough in range and large enough in number to cover the scope of the performances addressed by the assessment system in terms of representativeness and comprehensiveness and that permit valid inferences about performances to be made.

scale A continuum, such as scores possible on a test or individual performance task. The following describe several types of scales:

- Nominal (or naming) scales categorize by identity only (e.g., male and female, African American, Hispanic, Asian, and Native American).
- Ordinal (or ordering) scales are categorized by identity and order (e.g., a ranking such as 1st through 5th; a percentile). Most rubrics have ordinal scales.
- Interval scales are categorized by a fixed unit of measurement (e.g., temperature, age).
- Performance assessment items are typically scored on a four-point to six-point ordinal scale compared with a nominal scale of two (right/wrong or present/absent) on true/false items and checklists.

selected response items or tasks Items or tasks in which students select from among response or answer choices that are presented to them (e.g., true/false, matching, multiple choice).

sequential scoring A method of scoring in which there is a separate rubric or checklist for each standard demonstrated by the performance, each is applied to the performance, and each result is applied to the appropriate standard. For example, a task that assesses problem solving and concepts of functions would be scored sequentially using first a problem-solving rubric and then the rubric for concepts of functions.

simultaneous scoring The use of one rubric or checklist to provide information on more than one standard. This only occurs when the performance to be scored is the same in both standards, such as the inquiry process in science and mathematics.

standardization A set of consistent procedures for administering and scoring an assessment. The goal of standardization is to ensure that all students are assessed under uniform conditions so that interpretation of their performance is comparable and not influenced by differing conditions. Standardization is an important consideration if comparisons are to be made among scores of individuals or groups.

standards Statements that identify the essential knowledge and skills that should be taught and learned in school. Essential knowledge is what students should know. Essential knowledge includes the most important and enduring ideas, issues, dilemmas, principles, and concepts from the disciplines. Essential skills are what students should be able to do. Skills are ways of thinking, working, communicating, and investigating. Standards also identify behaviors and attitudes related to success in and outside of school. These include (but are not limited to) providing evidence to back up assertions and developing productive, satisfying relationships with others.

standards-based A descriptor that suggests how a clear and direct relationship exists among any combination of activities, materials, instructional processes, and assessments and that all relate to each other and to identified standards.

standards-based assessment Criterion-referenced assessment in which the criteria are taken directly from standards.

standards-based curriculum Curriculum designed with a specific focus on standards. Cumulatively, across all learning experiences and units of study, as well as their related assessments, all students have access to and demonstrate attainment of the knowledge and skills identified in the standards.

standards-based system A system in which the classroom curriculum is designed to help students attain defined standards. There is congruence among a focus on standards, the learning-teaching activities and materials selected to engage students, and the assessments used to document student attainment of the standards. Published materials, units of study, skill sequences, instructional experiences, routines or strategies, and assessments are standards-based only to the extent they link learners with standards within a classroom and across classrooms and grades, in a consistent and purposeful way.

standards-based unit of study A unit of study that is a combination of activities, materials, instructional processes, and assessments that relate directly to each other and to identified standards and that are designed to lead the student directly to the attainment of the identified standards.

standards-linked A descriptor suggesting that a process has taken place to determine that a relationship exists between identified standards and particular activities, materials, and assessments.

standards-referenced assessment Assessments that provide scores describing student performance against a set of standards rather than against the performance of other students.

summative assessment A snapshot of student performance at a given point in time, judged according to preestablished standards and criteria. Summative assessment typically leads to a status report on success or degree of proficiency.

task An activity, exercise, or problem given to the students to perform. The best tasks elicit multiple responses to a challenging question or problem and are aligned with one or more standards. For example, students write an essay, design an experiment, or solve a math problem.

task-specific rubric A set of scoring guidelines specific to a particular task. The criteria are addressed and described in terms of specific content or capacities that can be demonstrated in terms of particular, identified content relevant to the task.

test A set of items or situations designed to permit an inference about what a student knows or can do in one or more areas related to standards.

validity A measure of whether an assessment measures what it is intended to measure. For example, a valid assessment of mathematical problem solving would be to measure a student's ability to solve a problem, not merely the student's ability to read the problem.

Selected Resources

Erickson, H. L. (1998). *Concept-based curriculum and instruction: Teaching beyond the facts.* **Thousand Oaks, CA: Corwin Press.**

Design a seamless learning program that teaches students how to grasp broad concepts and integrate the information they learn. Erickson offers specific strategies for curriculum design, instruction, and evaluation to help create such a program. You'll find details on developing concept and process curriculum in a single discipline, in interdisciplinary units, and across grade levels. You'll also learn how to align your curriculum with state and national standards, generate "big idea" topics, and establish appropriate performance assessments.

Harris, D., & Carr, J. (1996). *How to use standards in the classroom.* **Alexandria, VA: Association for Supervision and Curriculum Development.**

How can you bring standards to life in your classroom? This guide is for teachers who seek a model for designing standards-based units of study to use in their classrooms. The authors share their experiences with standards-based learning and offer practical examples of how to develop standards into units of study. The model and processes they describe in this book help readers to choose and coordinate standards, topics, products and performances, assessment criteria, exemplars, and scoring guides.

Joyce, B. R., & Weil, M. (1996). *Models of teaching.* **NY: Allyn and Bacon.**

This book covers the rationale and research on the major well-researched models of teaching. The book also illustrates K–12 classroom use through scenarios and examples of instructional materials.

Marzano, R. J. (1992). *A different kind of classroom: Teaching with Dimensions of Learning.* **Alexandria, VA: Association for Supervision and Curriculum Development.**

This book describes the Dimensions of Learning program, a comprehensive K–12 instructional framework that teachers can use to improve the way they plan instruction, design curriculum, and assess student performance.

Mitchell, R., Willis, M., & The Chicago Teachers Union Quest Center. (1995). *Learning in overdrive: Designing curriculum, instruction, and assessment from standards.* **Golden, CO: North American Press.**

Developed by and for busy teachers, this book shows how to begin with standards to create rich units of instruction. Lists, forms, and samples provide tools to plan and implement interdisciplinary units.

Reeves, D. B. (1997). *Making standards work: How to implement standards-based assessments in the classroom, school, and district.* **Denver, CO: Center for Performance Assessment.**

Many states and districts are adopting new standards. Now what? The promise of the standards movement will accomplish nothing if it does not lead to changes in the classroom, school, and district. How do you transform standards into reality? This book is a full-length manual that tells you how to implement standards. The standards include a comprehensive, step-by-step approach, extensive appendices, checklists, glossary, bibliography, and sample assignments and assessments.

Wiggins, G. (1998). *Educative assessment: Designing assessments to inform and improve student performance.* **Jossey-Bass.**

Grant Wiggins outlines design standards for performance-based assessments that promise students—no matter what their ability—clear and worthy performance targets, useful feedback, coaching, and the opportunity to progress toward excellence. Educative Assessment furnishes the information needed to design performance-based assessments, craft performance tasks that meet rigorous educational standards, score assessments fairly, and structure and judge student portfolios. This book also shows how performance assessment can be used to improve curriculum and instruction, grading, reporting, and teacher accountability. In addition, the book includes numerous design templates and flowcharts, strategies for design and troubleshooting, and myriad examples of assessment tasks and scoring rubrics that Wiggins has developed and refined using feedback from clients in schools, districts, and state departments of education.

Wiggins, G., & McTighe, J. (1998). *Understanding by design.* **Alexandria, VA: Association for Supervision and Curriculum Development.**

Wiggins and McTighe provide an outstanding framework for curriculum design and assessment. They describe six "facets" of understanding that enable students to truly understand as the curriculum is "uncovered" rather than "covered." Advocating that you "begin with the end in mind," the authors describe a design process that is backward to what most people do. You begin with the desired end result, followed by the development of assessment activities, asking, "What would count as evidence of successful teaching?" Only after you do this do you begin to consider the design of units, activities, and actual plans. The book also includes helpful design tools that can be used throughout the process.

Bibliography

Addison Central Supervisory Union. (2000). *Profile of schools*. Middlebury, VT: Addison Central Supervisory Union. (http://www.acsu.k12.vt.us).

Addison Central Supervisory Union. (1999). *Student assessment plan*. Middlebury, VT: Addison Central Supervisory Union.

Connecticut Academy for Education in Mathematics, Science, & Technology, Inc. (1998). *Fourth annual survey on the use of educational time in Connecticut schools*. Middletown, CT: Connecticut Academy. (http://www.ctacad.org).

Danielson, C. (1996). *Enhancing professional practice: A framework for teaching*. Alexandria, VA: Association for Supervision and Curriculum Development.

Danielson, C., & McGreal, T. (2000). *Teacher evaluation to enhance professional practice*. Alexandria, VA: Association for Supervision and Curriculum Development.

English, F. W. (1992). *Deciding what to teach and test: Developing, aligning, and auditing the curriculum*. Thousand Oaks, CA: Corwin Press.

Essex Town Supervisory Union. (1998). *Essex Town Supervisory Union standards*. Essex, VT: Essex Town Supervisory Union.

Georgia Initiative on Math and Science. (1997). *Georgia framework for learning mathematics and science*. Athens: Georgia Initiative on Mathematics and Science.

Gross, K. I. (1999). *Vermont mathematics initiative: A summary prepared for the Vermont Senate Education Committee*. Unpublished.

Harris, D. (2000). *Pathways to Educational Understanding Education Initiative external evaluation*. Grand Isle, VT: The Center for Curriculum Renewal.

Harris, D. (1999, August 11). Unpublished interview with David Marsters, Montpelier, VT.

Harris, D., & Carr, J. (1996). *How to use standards in the classroom*. Alexandria, VA: Association for Supervision and Curriculum Development.

Herman, J. (1996). Technical quality matters. In R. E. Blum & J. A. Arter, *Handbook for student performance assessment*. Alexandria, VA: Association for Supervision and Curriculum Development.

Illinois Academy for Math and Science. *The physics of change*. Unpublished.

Lewis, A. C. (1998, Fall). Student work. *The journal of staff development*, pp. 24–27.

Lipton, L., & Wellman, B. (1998). *Pathways to understanding*. Guilford, VT: Pathways Publishing.

Lipton, L. & Wellman, B. (1999). *Data driven dialogue: A series for the Vermont Standards and Assessment Consortium*. Montpelier, VT. Unpublished materials.

Loucks-Horsley, S., Hewson, P. W., Love, N., & Stiles, K. E. (1998). *Designing professional development for teachers of science and mathematics*. Thousand Oaks, CA: Corwin Press.

Murphy, C. U. (1999, Spring). Use time for faculty study. *The*

Journal of Staff Development, pp. 20–24.

National Research Council. (1999). *Global perspectives for local action: Using TIMSS to improve U. S. science and math education.* Washington, DC: National Academy Press.

New Jersey State Board of Education. (1996). *New Jersey cross-content readiness standards.* Trenton: New Jersey State Board of Education.

Regional Lab of the Northeast and Islands. (1987). *Continuing to learn: A guidebook for professional development.* Andover, MA: Author.

Rosenstein, J. G. (1998). *FANS (Families Achieving the New Standards).* Trenton: New Jersey Math Coalition.

Schmoker, M. (1999). Results: The essential elements of improvement (workshop materials). Association for Supervision and Curriculum Development conference on Teaching and Learning, Reno, NV.

Schmoker, M. (1996). *Results: The key to continuous school improvement.* Alexandria, VA: Association for Supervision and Curriculum Development.

Stephenson, A. (2000). *The VISMT associates program.* Montpelier, VT: Vermont Institute for Science, Math, and Technology.

University of Chicago School Mathematics Project. (1995). *Everyday mathematics.* Chicago: Everyday Learning Corporation.

Vermont Department of Education. (1999). *School improvement support guide.* Montpelier, VT: Author. (http://data.ed.state.vt.us/apg/index.html).

Vermont Department of Education. (1996). *Vermont framework of standards and learning opportunities.* Montpelier, VT: Author.

Vermont Department of Education, & Vermont Institute for Science, Math and Technology. (1999). *Action planning guide.* Montpelier, VT: Vermont Department of Education.

Vermont Legislature. (1997). *Equal Educational Opportunity Act.* Montpelier, VT: State of Vermont.

Vermont Standards Board for Professional Educators. (1999). *Standards for Vermont educators: A vision for schooling.* Montpelier, VT: Vermont Department of Education.

Washington Central Supervisory Union. (2000). *Standards linking implementation plan.* Berlin, VT: Washington Central Supervisory Union.

Washington Partnership for Learning. (1999). *School improvement effort.* Washington Partnership for Learning.

Windsor Southwest Supervisory Union. (n.d.). *Windsor Southwest Supervisory Union: Supervision and evaluation procedures.* Chester, VT: Windsor Southwest Supervisory Union.

Acknowledgments

This book emerges from our experiences over the past several years supporting schools and districts in their work with standards-based learning. We have been fortunate to work with remarkable educators and their partners. Although it is not possible to list all of our wonderful colleagues, we wish to acknowledge the special contributions of the following leaders.

In Vermont, we thank the teachers, administrators, and partners of the Addison Central Supervisory Union, Chittenden South Supervisory Union, Essex Town School District, the Montpelier Public Schools, the South Burlington School District, the Washington Central Supervisory Union, and the Windsor Southwest Supervisory Union. These educators were willing to take the risk of exploring with us the opportunities and challenges inherent in standards-based curriculum, instruction, and assessment.

Thank you to colleagues and partners in the Los Angeles Unified School District; the Pathways to Education Understanding Project; the West Springfield, Massachusetts, School Department; the Middle Grades Lighthouse Project in South Carolina; and Intermediate Unit 3 in Pennsylvania.

We acknowledge the help and contributions of John Ferrara, Tim Flynn, Kerry Garber, Elaine Grainger, Marc Hull, Marge Petit, Sue Rigney, Doug Snow, Doug Walker, and David Wolk of the Vermont Department of Education; Ken Bergstrom of Goddard College; Nicole Pfister of the Flood Brook School in Londonderry, Vermont; and Matthew Joyce of Wilmington High School in Wilmington, Massachusetts. Without their vision, commitment to improving education for *all* students, questions, and sharing of materials and processes with us, there would be no standards-linking process. Many of the charts, diagrams, and tools included in this book originated in discussions with these fine colleagues.

In addition, we thank the colleagues and partners at the ASCD Assessment Consortium; Carnegie Middle Grades School State Policy Initiative; IBM Reinventing Education Initiative; National Gardening Association; National Science Foundation; Vermont Institute for Science, Math, and Technology; and Vermont Standards and Assessment Consortium.

Thank you to Paul Haskell of Ram Design for database development and technical support.

A special thanks to Nancy Herman, our colleague at the Center for Curriculum Renewal. Her questions, insight, and experience have a great deal to do with what has become the best of standards linking.

Finally, we thank Joyce McLeod, Nancy Modrak, John O'Neil, and Darcie Russell of the Association for Supervision and Curriculum Development for their enthusiasm, encouragement, and support.

Index

About the Authors

Judy F. Carr and Douglas E. Harris are Directors of the Center for Curriculum Renewal, a consulting group providing professional development and technical expertise in standards-based learning, leadership development, mentoring and colleague support, and building assessment and reporting systems to educators, associations, and businesses throughout North America. Contact them at 32 Chittenden Drive, Burlington, VT 05401. E-mail: CCRlearn@ aol.com. Phone: (802) 860-6802.

OUACHITA TECHNICAL COLLEGE

Related ASCD Resources: Standards

ASCD stock numbers are noted in parentheses.

CD-ROMs

Standards for Excellence in Education (#598337)
Standards Record-Keeping and Reporting (#500347 Windows; 501238 for Mac)
Standards ToolKit, 2nd edition (#599272)
Understanding Teaching: Implementing the NCTM Professional Standards for Teaching Mathe-matics (#597142 Windows; #597143 Mac)

Print Products

ASCD Inquiry Kit—*Implementing Standards-Based Education* (#999222)
ASCD Topic Pack—*Standards/National Standards* (#197199)
A Comprehensive Guide to Designing Standards-Based Districts, Schools, and Classrooms by Robert J. Marzano and John S. Kendall (#196215)
Content Knowledge: A Compendium of Standards and Benchmarks for K–12 Education, 3rd edition, by John S. Kendall and Robert J. Marzano (#100291)
How to Use Standards in the Classroom by Douglas E. Harris and Judy F. Carr, with Tim Flynn, Marge Petit, and Susan Rigney (#196197)
Standards for Excellence in Education: Guide for Parents, Teachers, and Educators (#198338)

Videotapes

Raising Achievement Through Standards (#498043, 3-tape series)
Science Standards: Making Them Work for You (#495241)
Using Standards to Improve Teaching and Learning (#400262, 3-tape series)

For additional resources, visit us on the World Wide Web (http://www.ascd.org), send an e-mail message to member@ascd.org, call the ASCD Service Center (1-800-933-ASCD or 703-578-9600, then press 2), send a fax to 703-575-5400, or write to Information Serv-ices, ASCD, 1703 N. Beauregard St., Alexandria, VA 22311-1714 USA.

OUACHITA TECHNICAL COLLEGE